A Stranger from the Past

Don Durrett

Copyright © 2010 by Donald David Durrett
All rights reserved.
(Fifth Edition – October 2023)

Library of Congress Control Number: 2010942442

No part of this book may be reproduced in any form or by any electronic or mechanical means including information storage and retrieval systems, without permission in writing from the author.

Cover & Book Design by EckoHouse Publishing

ISBN: 978-1-4276-5061-0

www.dondurrett.com

Books by Don Durrett

Conversations With an Immortal

Spirit Club

New Thinking for the New Age

Finding Your Soul

Last of the Gnostics

The Gathering

Ascension Training

Team Creator

The Path Forward

Get Healthy / Stay Healthy

America's Political Cold War

Post America: A New Constitution

The Demise of America

Introduction

This was my first book. I originally wrote it in 1990. This book is fiction and is not my vision or expectation of the future. The story is completely far-fetched and was used as a means for sharing ideas that were on my mind.

Until 1989, I had no idea what the word *metaphysics* meant. I was clueless, spiritually speaking. Then, in May 1989, I heard a lady on the radio claim she had communicated with Nostradamus. I believed her and bought her book. In that book, *Conversations with Nostradamus* by Dolores Cannon, Nostradamus states that our civilization is soon going to change dramatically. And that if we want an idea of what's going to replace it, we should look to the New Age movement in the American Southwest.

At that time, it was not apparent that massive changes were coming. However, today, you have to be extremely optimistic to ignore the trends of our time: looming oil and food shortages, debt at historical levels, perpetual wars, and a materialistic culture that only knows growth when growth is no longer possible.

We live in a period of great change, and economic malaise and social turmoil are becoming the new normal. Soon, there will not be enough food and oil to serve the global population. The problem of how to ration resources and keep our culture intact seems insurmountable.

Why are these incredible changes happening? The answer to that question is complicated, but I can give you the short answer. This current civilization is coming to an end. Just as Lemuria, Atlantis, and the Mayan civilizations ended, so will our present civilization. And just as there is no remaining evidence of Atlantis, there will be very little remnant of our present civilization. Not because we all died, but because we learned another way to live.

How much more time does the present civilization have? Well, the demise has already begun. By 2030, the world will have changed so much we will likely consider ourselves to be transitioning into a new era. And by 2050, we will no longer recognize vestiges of the past.

What is not recognized by most people today is the fact that we are now living in a transition period leading to a new civilization. We are on the cusp of the dawn of a new era. We are the generation that gets to experience its birth.

The changes will come now fast and furious. I've been on this journey now for over thirty years. During that time, the changes have come slowly, but they have occurred, and I see what's coming.

When Nostradamus said that the next civilization would be born from beliefs that New Agers hold, I had no idea what he was talking about. Now I do. They believe that there is only one consciousness which we all share. Guess what? It's true. You may not believe it, but your kids probably will. In fact, it will be the basis and foundation for the next civilization.

This fact – that we all share the same consciousness – changes everything. This is the truth that has been withheld from humanity. It is also the truth that sets us free. When it is first released to the public (my guess is around 2025), most won't believe it. However, since it is true, it will continue to be accepted. By the end of the decade, it will be well established and begin to impact humanity.

If we share the same consciousness, that means we are all family. In fact, it means we are all aspects of God. This fact ends religions. It also ends racism and cultural differences. It brings us all together. As I said earlier, it changes everything.

About 5% of the population knows the truth today – that we all share the same consciousness – and most of them are New Agers. Amazingly, this is exactly what Nostradamus told Dolores Cannon back in 1989. This percentage will now begin to expand rapidly. Then, as more people accept this truth, old belief systems will begin to break down. As a result, all of our social systems will experience radical change.

For example, everything you know about religion is probably wrong, and you can imagine the tumult necessary for those beliefs to go away! That is the type of change that is coming in the near future.

The purpose of my books is to help people prepare for what's coming. The transition will initially be harsh as society implodes before it begins to change into a better world. As a civilization, we are on a journey of learning that we are all one and discovering the inner being that is our true self. Those who initially come to this understanding and awareness will be the forebearers of the coming new era. You will be the ones who spread the word and spread your light.

Donald David Durrett
October 2023

Contents

Introduction vii

Prologue 1

Chapter One
San Antonio Prison 3

Chapter Two
The Underground 43

Chapter Three
Leaving the Prison 51

Chapter Four
Chicago 77

Chapter Five
The Speech 103

Chapter Six
Colorado 125

Prologue

A technician approached the entrance to a medical lab and positioned his eye for a retinal scan. He heard the familiar beep that granted access and waited for the door to open. As he walked through the door, he glanced down at his clipboard for the location of the patient. Row 23.

This lab was a location for thousands of cryogenically suspended human beings. It was more a warehouse than a lab. There were rows and rows of tubes, light blue in color and stacked three levels high. As the technician walked down Row 23, he glanced at the computer screens for each body. The screens stated the person's name, cryopreserved date, and revival date. Near the end of the row, he saw a dim flashing light, alerting him that a revival date had been reached.

He stopped at the tube and pressed a few buttons, bringing up the patient's history. "Strange," he thought, reading that the patient was cryopreserved at age 34, while completely healthy, in the 20th century. He had never revived anyone cryopreserved that long ago.

He pressed a few buttons, and the unthawing process began. Later in the day, he would retrieve the body so doctors could restart the patient's heart.

A Stranger from the Past

Chapter One

San Antonio Prison

I woke up in a hospital room. Something was wrong. I felt fine but had a strange feeling that I was in the future. I didn't recognize the hospital equipment. On one of the walls was a futuristic screen that showed my internal organs in vivid three dimensions. I know they were mine because when I moved, so did the images on the wall. How is that possible, I thought? Another monitor was flashing a series of graphs and numbers with what looked like my vital signs. Even the hospital bed was strange, made out of a material I did not recognize.

I wasn't awake long when they came for me. It was two Chinese soldiers and a woman doctor. She looked American but spoke Chinese in a perfect dialect. She pleaded with the soldiers, especially the one who appeared to be in charge. I couldn't understand what she was saying.

Finally, she gave up pleading, bowed slightly at the waist and abruptly left the room. Seconds later a nurse, who also looked American, came with a wheelchair for me. The soldiers stood at the base of my bed, and the nurse asked me to get into the wheelchair.

I never said a word to the soldiers, and I wasn't afraid. In fact, I was detached.

I calmly asked the nurse if I could ask a question.

She shook her head. "They are taking you now. There is no time. You were cryogenically frozen in 1994. Yesterday they revived you and restored your body back to a normal state. That's all I know."

Those were the only English words I heard at the hospital.

As the nurse wheeled me down the corridor, I wondered where I was. I wondered who *they* were and why I was unthawed. Strangely, I had no memory of going to the hospital to be cryogenically suspended. My last memories had nothing to do with being frozen. My last memory was going to bed after another normal workday. I wondered why or who had put me into suspension. I remembered being healthy and thought that only dead people were frozen in the 1990s.

The more I saw of the building, the more I was convinced I was in the future. It was subtle differences, such as the wheelchair itself. It was made of light plastic tubing, and the wheels were like Rollerblades. If the nurse would have pushed and let go, I would have zoomed down the hall and crashed into something.

As we approached the exit, I didn't see many people, but those I did see appeared to be American. They stared at me with an intense curiosity. What did they know about me? I wanted to talk. I wanted to ask someone where I was, but the soldiers were in charge. All I could do was remain silent.

Then we were outside. The buildings that I could see didn't look futuristic. In fact, they looked old and decrepit. My first reaction was recognition. This had to be future America. It was too similar not to be. It reminded me of a small town that had aged noticeably.

Chapter One - San Antonio Prison

The bus waiting in front wasn't an ordinary bus. But then, nothing about this place or my circumstances was ordinary. The bus was shaped somewhat like a missile. I had never seen anything like it. One of its distinct features was a lack of regular windows. The windows that circled the bus looked like small portholes on an airplane.

The door to the bus opened. Waiting for me were two more Chinese soldiers. As they escorted me down the aisle, I discovered this was a prison transfer bus. There were about 20 people on the bus, and were tethered to their seats. It was eerie. The other prisoners were silent and avoided my eyes. There was a palpable sense of fear in the entire bus.

At an empty seat, the two soldiers roughly strapped me down. My hands were free, but the straps prevented me from moving.

The other prisoners appeared to be Americans, like me. They were dressed in prison-issue blue jumpsuits, like the one I was wearing. That is why people had been staring at me in the hospital. I was a prisoner.

As the guards turned to go, they spoke to me in broken English, 'Do not talk. We will shoot you."

Now I understood the silence. I looked at the people around me. Few would meet my eyes. These men were terrified.

I wondered where they were taking us. The Chinese bus driver kept a busy eye on us through his rearview mirror. His two cohorts sat comfortably behind him, both armed and ready. Their job was easy to discern: keep a vigilant eye on us prisoners and their finger on the trigger.

Then the bus engine roared to life. The driver shifted into gear, and we began our journey.

As the bus drove through the small town, I tried to see as much as I could with the small windows restricting my view. I didn't see any people or any vehicles. The buildings were dated and uninhabited. Before long, we were at the edge of town and into a desert.

We drove for hours. I had the impression the bus was traveling much faster than 70 miles per hour. We were on an old highway, and there was no other traffic. The nondescript terrain of the desert swept past us in a blur. The bus never stopped.

Later that day, the guards fed us. We were given a bag of green chips and a cup of water. When we needed to use the restroom, we pushed a button on our seat, and were escorted to the restroom in the rear of the bus. On these occasions, I tried to look into the other prisoners' eyes. Few looked back. It was depressing. And so passed the night.

On the second day, the prisoner sitting next to me spoke as we drove through a decayed, uninhabited large city. "It's an ugly sight," he said. He was right. It looked as if looters had ravaged and vandalized the place, and then went on their way.

Continuing through the city was more of the same. We drove slowly, in order to avoid the potholes that dotted the road. There was no other traffic and no sign of life. It reminded me of a ghost town in old westerns, except this town once had been a modern metropolis.

Suddenly we were speeding away from the city. I turned my head to the porthole window. The sprawling, large city was definitely uninhabited. The skyscrapers that made up the skyline were like tombstones.

I turned back and gave an inquiring look to the person next to me. "Houston," he said in a somber voice and immediately looked away.

Chapter One - San Antonio Prison

I tried to engage him to talk again. At the risk of being shot, I whispered several questions but received no response. All I could do was look at the surroundings and wait. There were miles of strip malls from what looked like the 20th century yet were now ancient and decrepit. It was recognizable to me. Now I knew I was in the future.

A few hours later, someone gasped in the back of the bus. It was a sound I will never forget. The sound of horror. The man next to me was also afraid. He literally shook with fear. At first, I didn't understand. I looked out the window and noticed some odd-looking observation towers. I could not discern what they were, but they were large and at least 50 feet tall, with a glass-enclosed structure at the top. There was one tower every mile as far as I could see. The towers circled something. I couldn't tell what it was. But as we came closer, I understood. It was another city.

At the city outskirts, we encountered a large wall, 30 feet high and solid concrete. On top of this enormous wall, cameras were installed at regular intervals. We were approaching a huge prison.

After two days, the bus was finally stopping. It rolled to a stop in front of a large steel door that slowly opened. A prison entrance to what I presumed was hell. We drove through and the steel door closed behind us. We were surrounded by four walls and numerous security guards in a small courtyard. The walls were two stories high, which shaded the ground of dirt and a few weeds.

The Chinese guards wore military uniforms and were heavily armed. Several guards entered the bus and removed our bindings. They marched us to a one-way revolving door and ushered us into the prison, but they didn't accompany us.

Once through the revolving door, I could see a decayed city off in the distance, a few miles ahead. It was a city that should have had no inhabitants, yet it was populated with prisoners. The skyline was 10 miles away. The huge wall surrounding the city must have been 20 miles in diameter. I couldn't see a wall on the other side of the city, but I knew it was there.

We were unescorted, so I followed the others. They walked toward the skyline. We had no other choice. If we stayed there, we would die of thirst. A human body can only go a few days without water. Everyone was silent as if no words needed to be spoken. I kept my mouth shut.

After a few hours of walking, we approached the city. The few people we saw did not speak. Blank expressions masked their faces. The ragtag clothes they wore were filthy dirty and had not been washed in months. They looked near death, with hollow eyes, emaciated bodies, and smelled dreadful.

After another hour of walking, we started getting closer to the middle of the city and conditions seemed to be improving. Many of the people we now encountered were talking to each other, and their hygiene was not in such dire straits.

One of the members of our group was leading the way. We all deferred to him. He seemed to know where he was going. After hours of walking, we found ourselves in the streets of the old inner city. We passed under an arch leading to the downtown district. It was San Antonio.

The city was desolate. No electricity. No lights. All of the buildings were decrepit and decayed. In fact, most of the buildings were crumbling and dilapidated, with broken windows, dirt, and grime. The downtown streets

Chapter One - San Antonio Prison

were devoid of people, but I had the feeling of being watched.

Finally, we reached our destination. The man leading us approached a building and entered. The rest of us followed inside into a room full of people. I backed up against a wall and listened in sheer astonishment.

The group we found was unsightly. They wore grimy clothes and most hadn't washed their faces in weeks. The smell in the room was horrid, but the people present appeared articulate and intelligent.

A man seated at a table spoke to the man who had led us. He was evidently a leader among the prisoners. His clothes were a little bit cleaner, and he had an aura of strength that others respected.

"The death rate has been terrible. The dry food they feed us is crap. If you can't purchase anything on the black market, you're dead in a few years. They don't care. The Chinese want a high death rate so they can bring in more like us."

"I know how bad it is," replied the man who had led us. "We are ready to join the Underground and prepare for the day when we will be released. We might die here, but this prison can't last forever."

The local leader nodded. "Do you know all of the men who are with you?"

"All except one. We're ready to join. I'll take personal responsibility for these men." He paused and looked at me, against the wall. "Except him," he said, pointing at me.

The local leader looked at me for the first time since we had entered the room. Once his eyes met mine, his demeanor changed. "Who are you?" he commanded, in loud voice. I was obviously different from the others.

"I'm not sure," I said.

Suddenly tension filled the room.

He laughed. "Are you for real?" He looked over at the man who had led us. "Where did he come from?"

"We picked him up in the desert. At a hospital, in a small town outside Las Vegas. Hell, the rest of us came from detention centers, but not this guy. They wheeled him out in a wheelchair and escorted him onto the bus."

The local leader looked at me intently. "My name is Jackson. I'm one of the leaders of the Underground. The Underground controls the prison. We make the rules and we enforce the rules. If you value your life, you'll be straight with me. Do I make myself clear?"

I nodded.

He continued, "Now, what were you doing at that hospital, and who are you?"

I raised my eyebrows. "Do you want to talk in front of all these people?" I asked hesitantly.

"Come," he said, rising to his feet. Several of his companions accompanied us up some stairs. On the second floor, we found a sparse room with a dirty bed and several tattered chairs. After the door was closed, several of us sat down, and he nodded at me to begin.

"What year is this?" I asked.

"What year?" asked Jackson, bemused. "Are you kidding me?"

I shook my head. "One day I was in the 20th century. The next I was in some futuristic hospital, lying in a bed, wondering where I was."

The men all looked at each other. Finally, Jackson continued. "Tell us more."

"There isn't much to tell. Two days ago, I woke up in a hospital. There wasn't anyone in the room when I woke. I

Chapter One - San Antonio Prison

looked around and saw all of this bizarre equipment. I was definitely not in the 20th century. Anyway, I was lying in a hospital bed. Then two Chinese military officers came into my room with a doctor, a woman. She argued with them in Chinese. She was upset, but apparently didn't have much say in the matter. The next thing I knew, I was in a wheelchair heading for the exit. It happened fast."

Jackson scratched his thick beard and shook his head. "Hard to believe, my friend, hard to believe. But possible."

He paused when he saw my interest. I stared at him inquiringly.

"Yes, it is possible," he continued. "Around the year 2000, the old U.S. government started putting people into hibernation. Still, your story is difficult for me to accept. There's a man here who would be very interested in hearing about that period of history. I will take you to him."

Jackson paused, apparently having second thoughts. "What's the last date you remember?"

"January 11th, 1994 I remember it clearly. President Clinton was on a trip to Europe. The economy was doing well, and most people were happy."

Jackson looked at me. "Wow, that was a long time ago. Thinking back, maybe you didn't want to live through the next fifty years. That was a perilous time for the previous civilization. It was, perhaps, even worse than what we are now experiencing. We only know it from history, but it was a difficult time for people. More than two-thirds of the population perished."

Jackson rose from his seat. "Come, let's go see Anderson. He lives in the inner city. It will take us about an hour to get there."

I followed Jackson and his friends out of the building. We walked through the decrepit wasteland that was once San Antonio. An old 7-11 convenience store was barely recognizable by its battered sign.

"Jackson, see that building there, with the 7-ll sign?"

"Where?" he asked.

I pointed it out.

"Yeah, I see it. Why?"

"Do you know what it is?"

"I have no idea," he replied.

"It's a convenience store from the 20th century. Everyone wanted to save time. Convenience stores were like mini-grocery stores that didn't provide produce or meat. They provided speed. At a token increase in price, you could go into a convenience store and purchase an item in about one minute. The 7-11 stores were the king of convenience stores. There were thousands of them across the country."

Jackson laughed. "One minute? Today we have distribution centers, and we wait in line, and the centers only carry a few types of foods. Here in the prison, we are given dry food and water. On the outside, it's not much better."

He continued. "I've heard about the 20th century. A paradise compared to today. You lived during a period of affluence. Anderson will tell you what happened. He likes to talk."

The streets were empty. There were no automobiles or any other means of transportation, not even bicycles. Nothing but waste and debris. We were imprisoned in a desolate city with no resources.

Most of the buildings were empty, as well. I could see signs of life inside some of the buildings. People lived

Chapter One - San Antonio Prison

here. The people that we saw had hollow eyes and avoided our inquiring looks. They seemed to fear Jackson and his group.

Jackson stopped and looked at me to get my attention. "Anderson lives in a bad neighborhood. People have attempted to get him to move, but he has lived here for thirty years, and he hates change. The next couple of miles can be dangerous ..."

"I thought you were a leader of the Underground?" I interrupted. "Who is a threat to *you*?"

One of Jackson's friends laughed.

"We're the so-called good guys," Jackson said. "But there are other groups who have disassociated from our leadership. There are several Underground groups in the prison."

"Then each group has a different agenda?" I asked.

"It's more complicated than that. In general terms, that's true. We're all like gangs, and we only associate with our own group. Ask Anderson, he's much better at this than I am. Anyway, it can be dangerous here."

"What do you want me to do?" I asked.

"Stay with Olson." Jackson pointed to one of his friends. "He'll direct you, okay?"

I nodded.

"Olson and you will follow us at a short distance. We'll spot any trouble. If something happens, Olson will know what to do, okay?"

"Sure, let's go."

"You have a lot of nerve," Jackson said. "What's your name?"

"John."

"Johnson," he replied.

"Why Johnson?" I asked.

"The Chinese changed everyone's name. Today, everyone's name ends in *son*."

Jackson headed off down the desolate empty street with his group. Olson and I watched them go.

I asked Olson, "Do the Chinese make you keep your new names?"

He gave me a squeamish look and turned away.

"What's wrong? What did I say?"

"I don't like to talk, that's all."

I nodded.

Olson started walking, and I followed. We remained a half-block behind the others as we wound our way through the dilapidated streets. The road was once smooth asphalt, but now had potholes and cracks every few feet. It was evident none of the roads had any maintenance for decades, maybe centuries.

We were in an old, downtown business district. Uninhabited single-story buildings lined the streets. Olson moved along, hugging the buildings along the sidewalk. I followed by a few feet. The buildings were empty, except for thick dirt and grime and some old remnants of worthless furniture and debris. Many had broken windows.

Olson appeared to be relaxed. I didn't discern any fear in his demeanor. We followed the group slowly up the deserted streets, turning corners and heading up other streets. Each street was similar to the previous one. There was nothing here.

After several blocks, Jackson and his group stopped. Olson and I made our way to them.

"There isn't anyone in this sector today," Jackson said. "We're safe." He pointed to a building on the corner.

Chapter One - San Antonio Prison

"That's where Anderson lives. Come on, I'll take you to him."

Across the street, we approached an old American Savings & Loan. The door was steel. There were no windows.

"It's impossible to break in," Jackson said. "That's why Anderson lives here."

Jackson pushed an intercom. "Anderson, it's Jackson."

He turned to me. "He knows someone is at his door because he has an infrared security system. If anybody walks on this street, he knows about it."

After about 10 seconds, a voice came over the intercom. "Hello, Jackson, how are you today?"

"I'm fine. Listen, the sector is empty. Everything is quiet today. I have a guy here that I think you would like to meet. Open up, and I'll bring him in."

After a slight delay, the voice replied. "Jackson, are you sure it's safe?"

"Andy, I'm sure. This guy's on the level. No problem."

After a short pause, a buzzer went off, and Jackson pushed open the door. "Let's go," he said, nodding for me to follow. The two of us went inside. The rest of the group remained outside.

"Andy is paranoid," Jackson explained to me. "I'm his main contact in the local Underground, so he trusts me. He's lived here forever and doesn't like visitors. I'm probably the only guy who could have gotten you through that door."

The lobby was empty, except for beautiful white marble floors and walls. They were clean. Even the teller counter was dust-free. Who lived *here*?

Jackson went directly to an elevator, which surprised me because the building had only one floor. He pressed B for basement.

In the basement, a man was waiting for us. He was tall, thin, and clean-shaven, though his hair was long. He wore clean Levi's and an ironed, short-sleeved printed shirt. His distinct features would be easily remembered: a chin, square and larger than normal, and penetrating light blue eyes that exuded intelligence.

Jackson approached Anderson with a smile and shook his hand. "Andy, it's always a pleasure. Is everything fine? Do you need anything?"

Andy remained silent and cautious, staring at me. I followed Jackson, a few feet behind him.

"Who is this?" he demanded. Anderson was clearly Jackson's boss of some type. However, Jackson did not mind. In fact, I could tell that he liked Anderson and would do whatever he needed. The level of discourse was elevated in Anderson's presence, and Jackson liked to be around him. If there was a word to describe Anderson, it would be cultured, or perhaps classy. He had a dignified air about him.

"Andy, meet John. You are not going to believe where he's from," Jackson laughed.

"Jackson, please do not be so impetuous. I'm a busy man."

"Sorry, Andy," Jackson said, in a serious tone. "He came on the transport bus from Los Angeles today. I noticed something different about him. I asked a few questions, and he told me he's from the 20th century …"

"What?" Anderson interrupted. "What are you talking about?" Anderson glanced at me with a glare. This obviously sounded preposterous to him.

Chapter One - San Antonio Prison

I put my hand up to stop Jackson from answering. I took a step toward Anderson and extended my hand. "It's a pleasure to meet you." He shook my hand.

"Could we go sit down?" I asked. "And do you have something to drink? I've been walking for hours."

"Of course," Anderson replied curtly. He turned and walked away, and we followed.

The basement was beautifully furnished: thick carpeting on a polished hardwood floor, dark mahogany furniture, shiny brass lamps, and gorgeous framed prints on the walls. Impressive, even if there were no windows.

We went into his office. It was equally astonishing. The work desk was huge, though bare. The only substantial thing on it was a computer. On one wall, a series of bookshelves held at least a thousand volumes. The most striking thing about this room was the skylight. I stared, transfixed, at the skylight.

"I use mirrors to reflect the light throughout the day," Anderson said, relaxing a little.

"It's nice."

"Please sit down," he invited.

He sat behind his desk. Jackson and I sat in the two large, comfortable leather chairs in front of it.

Anderson pressed a button and shortly after a man appeared.

"This is my assistant, Peterson," Anderson said. "What would you like?"

"Water," I said. "Water will be fine, thank you." I thought of asking for food, but I didn't know what to ask for. What was dry food, anyway?

Anderson turned to Peterson. "Bring us some sandwiches, as well."

After Peterson left, Anderson turned to me. "Now, who are you?"

"Hmm. That isn't an easy question." I paused. "I'm still figuring that out. I was born in California in 1994. I had a wonderful childhood. Until I turned eighteen and graduated from high school, life was fairly easy and enjoyable. I had no problems and few responsibilities …"

"And America was prosperous," Anderson interjected. "Was your family?"

"Pretty much," I said. "We had a vacation home where I spent most of my summers. Anyway, after high school, life finally started. Until then, I didn't think about the future. High school graduation was a big shock to me, and I didn't know what to do. Society gave me, basically, two options: go to college or get a job. I chose a job, but it wasn't what I really wanted."

"What do you mean?" Anderson asked.

"Suddenly, life felt like a prison," I said. "I wasn't happy with my choices. In fact, I didn't feel like I had any choices. It was a period of my life where I was restless and uncommitted to any kind of ambition or achievement. I kind of dropped out, although I was working. In many respects, I was waiting for some kind of opportunity or direction."

"What happened next?" Anderson asked.

"I began changing. Previously, I had never looked at life in a philosophical way. Throughout childhood, I was never an exceptional student. I never tried very hard. My sisters were A students and were headed for college. Conversely, I was a C student who didn't do his homework. I rarely read anything besides the newspaper and magazines. Then, after high school, I started using my

Chapter One - San Antonio Prison

brain. Since I had rarely used it before, it was ready for some stimulation."

"You started reading more?" Anderson asked.

I nodded. "Growing up, I had always looked forward to the chase – the next party, the next pretty girl, the next sporting event. Life was a game, with few rules, and few responsibilities.

"But after high school, I realized that I couldn't play that game anymore. It was no longer fun. I had to find a new game, but what? I didn't have a clue. I knew that society didn't have the answer. Society said I should play their game, but I knew that would never satisfy me. Society wanted me to get married, go to church, pay my taxes, be a good citizen, and keep my mouth shut. I couldn't do that. I began looking for another game, something as exciting as the game of my youth, yet more satisfying."

"What did you find?" Anderson asked.

"I'm getting to it," I smiled. "After high school, I started looking for something, but I didn't know what. I worked for three years, but that was a dead end and wasn't giving me any answers. Society said that I could go to college, so I tried that. I went for seven years and received an advanced degree. I didn't go to college to get a better job. I was scheming. I was trying to understand society so that I could find answers. I wasn't looking for a way to improve society. I just wanted to understand it because that was the only way to find my way. It was only later when I became a closet anarchist, who wanted a better world. While I was searching for answers, I didn't like what America represented, and I didn't want to be part of it."

"Did you join any groups?" Anderson asked.

"Never, not one. I was scheming on my own. These were all my personal ideas."

"So, college helped you to think for yourself?" Anderson asked.

I nodded. "College was rewarding for me. It provided the opportunity to mature as a person and become educated. I left college a much better person. College sparked my interest in learning. And then, finally, I found something worth learning about. Actually, I found it when I was attending college, but not through a college course. It was my last year at college, in 1989.

"My new game was the meaning of life and metaphysics. I read a book called *Conversations With Nostradamus*. In the book, Nostradamus talked about how the New Age movement would become the foundation for the next civilization. He said that Christianity would wither away and be replaced by the principles of the New Age movement. At the time, I was a Christian, but Nostradamus' book rang true to me. I headed to the bookstore and found the New Age section. From then on, for the next few years, practically all I read was New Age material."

I paused.

Anderson stared at me, without saying a word. Then he stared at the floor in deep thought. After what seemed an eternity, he lifted his eyes. "How did you get here?"

"Three days ago, I woke up in a hospital. Instead of being told where I was, they put me on a bus that brought me here. The only thing I was told was that I had been unthawed. I have no memory of going to a hospital in 1994 to be frozen. The last day I remember is January 11th, 1994. As far as I remember, nothing eventful happened that day. My memory still thinks I'm in 1994."

Chapter One – San Antonio Prison

"Your story is possible," Anderson said. "I will try to find out what happened to you."

"How?" I asked. "I thought this prison was isolated from the outside world?"

Anderson smiled. He turned and looked at the array of monitors on the wall, then glanced back and raised his eyebrows. "I can find out." He paused. "I want you to stay with me," he said thoughtfully.

Next, he turned to Jackson and pointed at a table. "Jackson, there is a shipment coming next week. The date and time are on that table."

Jackson rose, went to the table, and found the directions. "Andy, is there anything else?"

"No, I will see you next week."

"Nice to meet you, Johnson. Good luck." Jackson smiled, waved, and walked out.

Anderson was finally smiling at me. "So, your new game was enlightenment? How did you play that game?"

I paused. "Can I ask some questions first? How did you come to live here? And I would like to know about the current state of the world and this prison."

"In time, John, in time. Please, I am interested in the game you found. Spirituality is my favorite subject. That and history are all I really care for. Don't worry. We'll talk about the world as it is now. First, I want to hear what you discovered."

I smiled at Anderson's enthusiasm. He was truly interested in what I had to say. I could now see that he was kind, and I trusted his sincerity. I felt comfortable in his presence, and I believed he had the answers to my questions.

"When I began looking for my new game, I never thought it would be a spiritual quest, but that's what it became. Once I began, I was consumed by it. I cannot overstate my focus. *Everything* I did was connected to my spiritual quest.

"I use the analogy of playing a game because that's how I perceived life when I was young. But I was looking for a new way to live, a new philosophy, and that was exactly what I found in spirituality. After that, my whole life became encompassed by my spirituality. Nothing was separate from my spiritual quest."

"What was this quest?" Anderson asked.

"To learn about God, the Creator, the Source of all. What questions haunt us from birth? *Who am I? Where did I come from? Where do I go when I die? What is the meaning of life?* These questions became the focal point of my quest. At first, I was amazed at the quantity of knowledge available. After a while, I learned that spirituality isn't for everyone, at least not the answers to these questions. The early 1990s were a good time to look for spiritual answers. I found source after source.

"I found out that I'm a fifth-level old soul priest-scholar. It was my destiny to seek the answers to these questions. More importantly, being an old soul, I had the ability to grasp the answers. Younger souls aren't ready for these answers. I was ready, and I absorbed it.

"Steadily, I was exposed to deeper and deeper layers of knowledge, and answers were revealed to me. In fact, the answers were available to anyone who looked hard enough, but you had to look. Most of this knowledge is hidden from the general public.

"For instance, in the early 1990s, only about three percent of the global population knew the truth. It was there to be found. In fact, it was hidden in plain sight. You said earlier that you study spirituality, so you should know the truth, which is that there is only one consciousness, which we all share."

I paused, grabbed a sandwich off the table, and took a bite as I leaned back in my chair. I was actually happy. I didn't know what was happening, but I trusted the universe and knew that I was an eternal soul and that whatever was happening, I had created for my benefit. I also knew that I wasn't alone. I knew that Joe, my spirit guide, was with me. I glanced around Anderson's office and wondered where he'd found his furniture. As I ate my sandwich, I stared at a beautiful painting.

"What is this?" I asked, pointing to the painting.

"That's from the future. A print from the Wingmakers. The painter is unknown."

"What do you mean, it's from the future?"

"I'll tell you about it later. The Wingmakers are time travelers. They brought us some of their artwork, as well as other materials from their civilization."

"Tell me more."

"Later. First, tell me the meaning of life?"

I smiled. "You don't know?"

"I would like to hear your opinion."

"What year is this?"

"2272."

"My God! You mean this planet is still spiritually in the dark? What happened to the Great Shift? How many know that God is *All That Is*?" I was concerned.

Anderson took a breath and blew out a long sigh. "I'm sorry, I didn't mean to mislead you. Many are aware that God is All That Is, at least fifteen percent. Many more are coming to accept it every day. Spirituality is flourishing around the world. I just want to hear it from you. I want to hear your views."

Anderson's sincerity was so heartfelt that I didn't ask any of the questions that were flooding my mind.

"Okay, I'll tell you. The meaning of life is simple: To be. We are here to learn, to expand our spirit, but, more importantly, to be representatives of God. Our bodies are nothing more than suits. After this life, we leave the suit behind. The experience … that we take with us.

"It is much more complicated than that, of course. I could talk about this for hours. In a nutshell, the meaning of life is simply *to be*. We don't have to learn. We don't need to achieve. We only need to be. The reason is that we are perfect manifestations of God already.

"Some say the meaning of life is life itself. Others say the meaning is to evolve the soul. I say it's simply to be. To be the manifestation of God. Yes, our souls are evolving, but they don't necessarily have to evolve. God is already perfect."

Anderson was visibly stunned. He rose from his chair and marched around the room, as if distraught. "You say this with such nonchalance. How well do you understand it? Do you realize that only a few people understood this in the 20th century?"

"No, no. There were many who knew. At least three percent of the population in 1994 was spiritually aware."

"How much do you know?"

"I learned a lot. As I told you, it was my game."

"Please, tell me more."

I grabbed another sandwich and leaned back in the chair in front of his desk. "Okay, I'll talk, but after I'm finished, you have to answer my questions. You have to tell me about history and the current civilization. I presume this should be easy, since you're a historian?"

Chapter One - San Antonio Prison

Anderson smiled. "We have plenty of time. I have more information than you can imagine. Don't worry, John, I have everything you need."

I smiled. "Where to begin? I'll just start talking. I've made two points so far: God is *All That Is*, and that the meaning of life is *to be*. Let me talk about those two concepts.

"Everything is God, *everything*. This chair, the air that we breathe, the cells in our body, our soul, everything. This is why God is referred to as *All That Is*. What does this imply? First, that we *are* God, and there is no separation between God and us. In fact, there is no separation between us and anything or anyone else. Everything is connected by consciousness. Everything is *one* consciousness.

"Everything is interrelated because everything *is* God. God is the whole, and everything else makes up the whole. Thus, our souls are pieces of God. An important point to understand is that each piece of the whole is as important as the next. To God, it's the *whole* that is important. To God, all pieces make a circle. If one piece is taken out, the circle is broken, and it is no longer a circle. Thus, each link is as important as the next."

Anderson rose from his chair and walked around the room in contemplation. "Why is the meaning of life *to be*?"

"Because the whole is just as alive as we are," I said slowly and deliberately. I paused and then said emphatically, "The whole is alive! The whole is one big consciousness, of which we are a part. The whole is not a being, separate from us. We are part of it! We are *being* God."

Anderson stopped and leaned against the bookcase. He nodded. "Yeah, we are being …. Keep explaining. I'm enjoying this."

"Think in terms of connections. We are connected to the whole, and we are connected to everything we perceive. Enlightenment is *knowing* that we are part of the whole. This is called *I AM* awareness. It's a realization that we are one with God, and so is everything else. 'I am God.' When we come to this realization, our perceptions change dramatically. We view the world from a new perspective: spiritual awareness.

"The whole is a consciousness in which everything interrelates. In effect, everything is alive and interrelated with everything else. For instance, our thoughts influence everything around us, and our thoughts create our reality ..."

Anderson interjected. "If our thoughts permeate among all consciousness, then our thoughts affect plants, animals, and especially people."

I nodded. "Exactly. The planet is a mass consciousness in which all thoughts influence each other. This mass consciousness provides us with experience. We provide the input through our beliefs, and the mass consciousness provides the output, which is our experience. Thus, we can experience only what the mass consciousness allows, and we can't escape its influence.

"The mass consciousness doesn't care how we live from a moral standpoint. Our beliefs can be whatever we want. The mass consciousness is like a giant computer taking our input and producing output. The mass consciousness provides our possible experiences: our choices. There are no right or wrong choices. What we select is perfect. So, we can choose whatever we want. And if we want to destroy the planet, that is our prerogative. This is a planet of free will."

"Wait," Anderson said. "Are you saying God doesn't care about morality?"

"First of all, morality only exists on the physical plane, and the physical plane is not real. This is all an illusion. It is just energy vibrating. Even our ego is fake. Everything is fake, including morality. If you begin to wrap your head around that, then you will begin to understand who you are.

"Morality and perfection cannot coexist. Morality is simply an idea, and ideas can change. God does not change. God exists as universal laws, such as the truth is always true. Object truth does exist. In fact, the only truth is objective.

"Morality only exists because we create it as a means for soul expansion, and so that God can experience the infinite. Without experiencing light and dark, life would be limiting. And one of God's universal laws is unlimitedness.

"Morality is a fascinating subject. Here is one way to understand it. God's core and our soul's core is love. When we perpetrate immoral acts during an incarnation by using our free will, our core knows that this is incongruent with love. So, when this lifetime is over, and we return home to the etheric spiritual planes, we make plans to move beyond immorality and to find our way back to love since that is our true self. So, God does have a built-in mechanism that leads us back to love if we behave badly. And trust me, we all behave badly from time to time."

Anderson nodded. "What are the universal laws of God?"

"That would take hours to explain. I'll give you one: unconditional love. God, or the whole, uses unconditional love as the guideline to create our experience. All experiences are created with the intent of learning about unconditional love. Each experience we have is co-created with God, and thus perfect."

Anderson squinted. "That's quite a statement. If true, how does that impact our free will? If God is co-creating with us, doesn't that imply that God's will is interjected into our lives?"

"The concept of free will is misleading. God is always with us, constantly co-creating our experience with us. There is never a moment when God is not aware of our thoughts, and these thoughts are recorded in the Akashic records. Everything we do and think is recorded. You can playback your life after this lifetime is over. But I digress. We do not have a separate identity apart from God. Likewise, we are connected to the mass consciousness. We cannot have an experience that the mass consciousness does not agree upon."

Anderson looked puzzled. He moved away from the bookcase and came back to his chair. "Earlier, I thought you said this is a planet of free will and that the mass consciousness allows us to choose our experiences, whatever they may be. If we're allowed to choose, isn't that free will?"

"On the surface, it may appear to be free will. But when you look below, you can see that everything is orchestrated. Choices are limited because of the integration of consciousness as well as God's universal law that everyone is learning about unconditional love. The foundation of life is love. That is the one constant in the universe. Once you understand that, you can understand God's nature as well as your own."

Anderson nodded. "I get it. God controls the integration with the intent that everyone learns about unconditional love. That implies that all of life's lessons are truly about unconditional love."

I smiled. "Very good."

"I'm still a little bit confused about free will and the ability to do as we choose."

"Think of it this way," I said, stretching my neck from side to side. "God gives us an incredible amount of leeway to decide which experiences we want to use to learn our lessons. We choose our experiences, but at the same time, God knows what we need to learn these lessons. And because we are all learning together, God makes sure the lessons focus on unconditional love, which eventually leads to spiritual awareness."

Anderson paused while contemplating. "Since we are all at different levels of spiritual awareness, does that mean we each have a different degree of free will? In other words, does God control some people's behavior more than others?"

I smiled. "Excellent question. I like the way you think. To a certain degree, that's true, but it's not exactly the right question. The answer is that we limit our choices before we incarnate. We curtail our own freedom. What must be understood is that God is intricately involved in selecting our experiences. God realizes that spiritual awareness is the objective. God is relentless in steering us toward enlightenment."

Anderson had a sudden epiphany. "I just realized something. Most people today think freedom is the most important thing we should pursue. But that's not true. It's the relationship with God that matters most, which we experience by our relationships with our fellow souls, even our enemies."

I clapped. "Excellent."

Anderson continued. "God created us to experience and learn about God, which is unconditional love. Our lives are a process of remembering who we are. We live one life after another, until we remember. As the saying goes, we live and learn."

I smiled. "Anderson, I'm glad I met you. I can see that you are a true student of metaphysics, and someone I can talk with about these subjects."

Anderson smiled. "Thanks, and if you'll indulge me, I would like to hear more about free will."

"You seem to have a pretty good grasp of the subject."

He leaned back in his chair. "Just a few more minutes."

I took another bite of my sandwich. "Okay, a few more minutes. God allows us free will to choose our experiences, but God makes sure that each experience provides spiritual growth in some way. Thus, we are always learning, and the mass consciousness is always evolving, with unconditional love and harmony as the objectives. So, when we are co-creating with God, God knows that unconditional love and harmony are destined in the long run. Even when we choose negative experiences, such as inflicting emotional pain upon another, the result is eventual growth. That negative experience will eventually lead us to unconditional love.

"Just look at our lives. Very few of us are saints, but we are all learning. Earth is an incredible classroom. Why? Because to know joy, we must experience sorrow. To know love, we must experience hate. This is how we learn our lessons. The good news is that as much hate and spiritual ignorance as there is on this planet, the mass consciousness is still working toward spiritual awareness and harmony. And, in the end, spiritual awareness and harmony *always* win."

Anderson interrupted. "Okay, let me see if I understand this. The mass consciousness lets us experience anger, hatred, and the gamut of negative emotions. But in the end, the mass consciousness brings us together into some kind of nirvana where harmony and spiritual awareness rule the day?"

I nodded. "It's inevitable over long periods of time because our core is love. As individuals, every life provides spiritual growth. Rarely do we regress, and even then, we learn lessons along the way. It is no different for planets. This planet's mass consciousness is growing spiritually, just like each of us."

Anderson squinted. "And somehow our individual lessons integrate with the spiritual evolution of the planet?"

I nodded. "The mass consciousness is the foundation from which lessons are made available. As the planet evolves spiritually, the lessons change to spiritual lessons. When we incarnate, we come to help the planet evolve. In fact, that is the prime objective for many souls.

"No one incarnates without planning in advance how they will live their life, and this planning process is done with God. Thus, God is aware of our plan. In fact, God doesn't ignore us for a single moment. God is right there with each and every one of us, involved in the planning of our lives. No one is ever alone or separate.

"God follows our every thought to help us on our path. God watches our back, because we are part of God. That's what co-creation is all about. Free will is largely an illusion. We are part of the whole, and we can't truly be free if we are part of a whole. Our individuality is an illusion. It is the whole that is the reality."

Anderson nodded. "I understand what you're saying about free will and how everything is interrelated, but what happens if we fall off the path and ignore the lessons we came to learn?"

"If we fall off the path, God teaches us something else. The further from the path we get, the more God becomes involved in our life. We actually lose our free will when we leave our chosen path. When we are in harmony with God, our free will is at its height, and much more flexible. For instance, have you noticed how people whose lives go downhill seem to never turn around? Whereas people who are successful tend to do many amazing things.

"When you are in alignment with God, you have more power. And when you are not, you lose that power. I'm not talking about power over other people, but the power to manifest what you want.

"The mass consciousness knows what we have planned, and also knows our previous and future lives. The mass consciousness is intricately involved in our experiences. It will either support us or hinder us. So, free will is really about being in alignment with what came to do. Everyone has a blueprint, which is their life plan.

"So, tell me, Anderson, after hearing me explain free will, do you feel free? Do you think you can do something without God being aware of it? Or, something that is contrary to your life plan?"

Anderson raised his eyebrows. "I don't know. I suppose God is aware of my thoughts and actions. What you say definitely implies that our free will is an illusion. It's disconcerting, in a way. It feels like life is fated."

I smiled, stretching my neck. "But it also implies that we have nothing to fear. If the whole is watching out for our welfare, because it is the whole's welfare as well, then we have nothing to fear. Don't you agree?"

Anderson nodded.

"I think that's enough for now. It's your turn."

"Were you a writer?" he asked. "Did you ever write any of this down?"

"Yes and no. I was not a professional writer. I tried to get published, but I was unsuccessful. I did write stories about the future in a spiritual context. I did write about my beliefs."

Anderson looked away and reflected, then turned back. "You may have been published. What's your last name?"

"Randall."

Anderson rose from his chair and walked across the room to the shelves of books. He returned with one and handed it to me with a smile. "Surprise."

I looked at the cover. My name was under the title. I opened it to see what year it was published: 2003.

"At the beginning of the 21st century," Anderson said, "many people began reading metaphysics after the 9/11 terrorist attack. A new spirituality was inspired by the New Age movement that began in the late 20th century. I suppose the popularity of metaphysics caused your book to make it into the hands of a publisher."

I stared at Anderson. "I need answers," I said impatiently. "I need to know where I am, who you are, and what happened to the world."

I was confident Anderson would tell me what I needed to know and that everything would work out. But I was ready to hear him tell me about this new world where I found myself.

He put up his right hand. "Okay, okay, sorry. I wanted to make sure you are who I think you are."

"What does that mean?" I asked, intrigued.

"There is a prophecy that you fulfill. A stranger from the past is supposed to come and lead us to freedom. The stranger is supposed to be enlightened."

I stared at Anderson. "Who is the source of this prophecy?"

"It was channeled through a man named Bradley Adams. He published a book titled *The Future of America*. It's a classic and widely known by the Underground. Many people believe in the prophecy."

"Do you take it seriously?" I asked.

"Now that I've met you, I do."

"Is the book here?"

"Yes."

"Good. I'll read it later, and then we can discuss it." I paused. "Okay, I'm ready for answers."

"A lot has happened since 1994. So, let's take it from the beginning.

"Shortly before you went into hibernation, Iraq invaded Kuwait. America decided that they couldn't allow this naked aggression and went to war against Iraq. America was protecting its oil interests and economy. As you know, America's foreign policy was focused on economic interests, and oil was the lifeblood of the economy. Anyway, Iraq was overmatched, and America annihilated its army in short order. Nearly a hundred thousand Iraqis died, and Iraq was bombed badly. America suffered fewer than one hundred casualties.

"That war destroyed the fragile stability of the Middle East. At the time, no one had any inclination of this fact, but it was only a matter of time before the Arabs sought

Chapter One – San Antonio Prison

their revenge against the 'infidels.' Less than a decade later, America was stuck in an endless war on terrorism.

"In 2023, the Arabs made their ultimate bid for revenge. It was a nuclear war. Israel was destroyed. Iraq and Iran were badly damaged. The Middle East was a battlefield for a couple of years. After the war, the world economy collapsed, which provided a means for China to become a world power.

"In 2032, China invaded the United States. They quickly won the war and took over the world. It's more complicated than that, much more complicated. I have a lot of literature on the past three hundred years. You can read as much as you want."

"The Chinese have been in control since 2032?" I asked.

Anderson nodded. "Since then, the Chinese have systematically destroyed our culture and suppressed our freedom. We no longer have an entertainment industry or professional sports. There are no more national parks or vacation resorts. Even our museums and history have been destroyed. They built huge prisons out of cities and locked away the nonconformists. All of our precious freedoms and individual rights were taken away. Today, the Chinese treat America as an economic fiefdom. They grow food and export it at incredible profits. Food crops are their major economic resource. They also have manufacturing plants throughout the country.

"The Chinese don't like Americans, and they decided to get rid of most of us. It was easy after the war. Famine and disease killed people by the millions. There's no proof, but many scientists today believe the diseases were intentionally released on the population.

"By the year 2100, there were only sixty million Americans left. The majority congregated in major cities where there was food. The Chinese isolated everyone. Traveling was nearly impossible, and still is. The country is a wasteland."

"Is there freedom anywhere on the planet?" I asked.

"Sure. Many countries are still democratic and free. That's where the Chinese sell their food. South America is generally democratic, and these countries have dynamic economies, especially Brazil. The rest of the world is generally under dictatorship, with faltering economies. Another exception is Australia. Australia is the new America, where everyone wants to live.

"Every country has had food shortages. As it turned out, a new ice age adversely impacted weather systems. It started getting colder around 2025 and progressed rapidly. The northern latitude countries became uninhabitable, and people had to migrate south. The cold weather has impacted food production severely in most countries. Australia has been an exception. Australia is steadily becoming a major power because of agriculture …"

"How long have you been here in this prison?" I interrupted.

He smiled. "That's the first time you have shown any fear. Are you asking me if you can expect to ever leave?"

I didn't answer.

He rose from his chair. "Come, I want to show you something." He started walking out of the room, and I followed. In the elevator, he pressed a button, and the elevator went *down*.

I was surprised. I hadn't expected another level below the basement.

Chapter One - San Antonio Prison

The elevator door opened, and we stepped out. Anderson was full of surprises. The floor above was his living quarters. This space was where he worked, and by the looks of the room, Anderson was working on something important. Maps covered the walls. The maps were marked with colored pens and numerous pushpins at various locations. Several large monitors were inset into the wall, and several computers hummed on the floor, indicating a large operation.

Anderson crossed the room to a wall covered by bookshelves filled with magazines, newspapers, and books. I followed. He found what he was looking for and handed it to me. A small trade journal with the title Underground. I looked at the date. It was printed in 2272, *this* year.

"That's the publication by the Underground," Anderson said. "Turn to page forty-four."

I turned to the page, an article about Omaha, Nebraska. I looked at the name of the author, J. L. Anderson. "Is that you?"

"Yes, I am J. L. Anderson."

"You wrote this article from here?"

"Yes."

"Then you have current information about Omaha?"

He nodded.

"So, you have contacts with the Underground on the outside?"

He nodded again.

"What is the Underground?"

"It's a group of people, like me, who refuse to give up. The Underground is the only organized opposition to Chinese rule. We will continue to do whatever it takes to regain our country. We've been active since 2032 when

America was invaded. The Underground has an extensive history, mostly failure, but today we are stronger than ever. That's mainly due to help from outside countries. For example, all of my electronics came from our foreign supporters, and our publication is printed outside this country. The Underground is getting stronger and stronger. It's because of our outside support."

"Jackson told me that you were part of the Underground in the prison."

"No, we're different groups. Let me explain. The Underground has been around since the Chinese invaded America over two hundred years ago. So, anyone who is a resister considers themself as part of the Underground. Thus, there are many groups, and not all of them are affiliated. The Underground in the prison is organized to govern the prison. I'm affiliated with what could be considered the real Underground."

"What about all of this equipment?" I pointed to the computers. "I heard you tell Jackson you're expecting a shipment. Do most of your possessions come from the outside? If they can smuggle items to you, they must be able to help prisoners in some way?"

"Sit down," Anderson said.

We sat at a table. I looked at the maps on the wall. They appeared to be cities and areas throughout what was once the United States.

"Earlier, you asked who I was," Anderson said. "I'm one of the leaders of the real Underground. I chose to come here nearly thirty years ago. I came here by choice because it's the safest place for me. I've lived here for the sole purpose of supporting the Underground. I can leave anytime. The same way my shipments arrive, I can leave.

Chapter One – San Antonio Prison

But I choose to stay. I can accomplish as much here as on the outside, and I feel safer here.

"As far as helping the prisoners, it would be self-defeating. The current sanctuary the prisons provide would be jeopardized. For this reason, the shipments are brought only here and are not dispersed.

"The Chinese built this prison over one hundred years ago, and they have built several others like it throughout America. They've never yet gone inside any of them, and they've never used spies to check up on the prisoners. Instead, they create such deplorable living conditions that they expect everyone on the inside to die within five years, which is the average lifespan on the inside. There is no sanitation or healthcare. The water is dirty and in short supply. As long as the death rate is high, the Chinese don't care what goes on inside."

"Who buries the dead and does routine jobs like that?" I asked.

"Jackson's group sees to it. They also pick up food and water at a designated gate near the wall."

I nodded.

"We of the real Underground want to make sure that the hands-off policy is maintained. Several other Underground leaders, like myself, are inside the prisons. We've used the prisons effectively as a cover. It's as safe here, if not safer, than anywhere on the outside. The outside is filled with spies and government informants. Most of my communications are with Underground leaders in other prisons or with our foreign supporters. All of my communication is done using satellites owned by foreign countries. It's very dangerous to have electronics on the outside. Most Underground communication on the outside is person to person.

"The prison system is the heart of the Underground. We coordinate activities and maintain control of our members from here. If it weren't for the prisons, we wouldn't have the cohesiveness and coordination that exists.

"Let me give you an idea of how the Underground communicates. First, several of us communicate electronically using foreign satellites and initiate a message using email. Next, people start contacting each other, person to person. We can spread a message across the country in a matter of days. The prison system provides the backbone for our organization.

"Lately, we have been exchanging emails about the discord that has arisen within the Underground. We are trying to figure out how to close this chasm and get everyone back on the same strategy of non-violence. That's another story we can discuss later.

"San Antonio is a tight prison because of its geographic location. It's in the middle of nowhere. It's difficult to move people or shipments in and out. I've had only three visitors from the outside in the thirty years I've been here. Other prisons are not as geographically isolated, and people move freely in and out."

Anderson paused. "It's time to eat and get some rest. Tomorrow we'll talk more. I want you to begin reading. I have an extensive library, with enough material for you to understand what has happened in the last three hundred years. I even have material about the period you came from."

As we walked back to the elevator, all I could think of was dry food. Before I was cryopreserved, I made an effort to eat healthy. Now I wake up, and they are feeding people food with little nutritional content and keeping the ingredients a secret. This was nothing more than human cruelty and an affront to human rights.

A Stranger from the Past

Chapter Two

The Underground

Dinner was not dry food. Anderson received shipments of food from the outside. He told me that dry food was a synthetic food made of soybeans, kelp, algae, and other secret ingredients. He said it lacked the proper nutritional requirements and left people malnourished. While people could live for several years on dry food, eventually it led to a premature death.

Before going to sleep, I read the article Anderson had written for the Underground publication. It was basically about politics, in which he outlined the current Chinese government policies and argued why these practices were intolerable.

Omaha, I learned, was the new financial hub of the nation. Banks and other financial institutions relocated there from New York in 2039 when a tectonic earth shift caused ocean water to flood large portions of the country. Omaha was one of the few places with a semblance of normal everyday life. This was possible because the financial districts provided jobs for both Americans and Chinese.

Fortunately for the Americans, the Chinese valued their services. They could have imported Chinese workers by the thousands but chose to use Americans. Tens of thousands of Americans worked in Omaha, mainly in financial services and international trade.

Everyone who wasn't Chinese had an NP (Native Population) designation. All NPs were required to have invisible identification tattoos stamped on the back of their hands. These tattoos were scanned through monitoring devices, which were everywhere. NPs were scanned many times per day when they boarded public transportation, when they went inside a public building, when they purchased something, and even when they left home. It reminded me of the tracking systems that Federal Express and UPS used in the 20th century to keep track of packages.

The NPs in Omaha were separated into various classes of people. The class with the highest status worked closely with the Chinese and was given special privileges. Below the top class were the upper management employees who had higher salaries and nicer living quarters. The lower class was the remaining workers. This working-class group was stripped of their rights and most privileges. But no matter how high a person's status, he or she was still an NP to the Chinese. NP might as well have meant you were a non-person. Even the few thousand privileged NPs were confined to Omaha and faced the same array of NP restrictions. For example, they were subjected to curfews, and their homes were electronically bugged. They also didn't have access to the same food as the Chinese (though they rarely ate dry food). Thus, even life for the elite NP was rigid, tightly controlled, and lacked all appearance of freedom.

All NPs were carefully indoctrinated and socialized. People were told how to live and what was acceptable. The Chinese monitored everyone, like in George Orwell's classic novel, *1984*. Children were expected to tattle on

Chapter Two - The Underground

their parents for any infraction, and workers were expected to expose their colleagues for crimes against the state. Any form of rebellion or political involvement landed a person in one of the barbaric prisons, which amounted to a death sentence. The population was carefully monitored, and anything out of the ordinary was scrutinized. The oppressors showed no compassion. Americans weren't allowed to have problems. They were treated like animals and expected to behave.

The Chinese immigrants were even more strictly monitored. Any deviation from state protocol and laws was met with swift retribution. They were killed by lethal injection, and they quietly disappeared. There were no prisons for the Chinese, only needles. Needles weren't used on NPs, because the prisons were more effective at maintaining control. The NPs were passive, and the Chinese wanted to keep it that way.

Reading about the current state of affairs was sobering and disconcerting. I wondered how the spiritual evolvement of the planet got so off-kilter, and what could be done to end the state of repression. It was evident that human rights were being violated and that change was needed.

The next morning, I joined Anderson for breakfast. We drank coffee and ate cold cereal. He said that besides his assistant and us, nobody inside the prison had access to any food other than dry food.

He said he had made a decision last night. I would be staying with him for a few weeks. He wanted me to tell him about the era in which I had lived, and he wanted me to understand the historical period I had slept through. After I got ready, he said we would be leaving.

"Where are we going?" I asked.

"On an important mission. The dissension in the Underground that I mentioned last night needs to be resolved. I've been telling myself for the last few years that I'm powerless to close the chasm that's been spreading. Now that I have met you, I think the two of us can make a difference."

Anderson paused. He wanted me to know the enormity of his decision. I didn't interrupt him. If he was going to take me out of this prison, I was going to help him.

He continued. "The discord relates to the age-old question of how to overthrow an oppressor? Because of the New Age movement that began during your lifetime, we are peaceful dissenters. We believe that love is the answer. We believe if we love each other, God will hear our call and remove the oppressor.

"The Bible says, 'resist not evil' and explains that we learn from adversity. The Underground's sole mission is to remain true to God. We acknowledge that God is aware of our plight and will find a peaceful resolution."

Anderson continued. "This peaceful approach requires incredible patience. As you are now aware, the Chinese have been in control for over two hundred years, and we've been using a strategy of non-violence the entire time. Our path has been to become more spiritual and learn to love our enemy. We spread the word of God, and we wait. The New Age movement doesn't advocate forcing our will upon another. We don't believe in the morality of violence. According to our spiritual concepts, war is fruitless."

"It sounds like spirituality has advanced quite a bit in the last two hundred years," I said. "The Underground

Chapter Two - The Underground

sounds like a spiritual movement to me. Why didn't you tell me before?"

"I'm sorry, I should have. Yes, it is a spiritual movement. We're trying to advance spiritually so that we can have peace on Earth. We decided years ago that this was the best course of action.

"Lately, a few young souls have become increasingly strident. They are openly calling for a militaristic approach. They want to become terrorists. Already, there have been a few incidents. A couple of months ago, a Chinese official was assassinated in Omaha. No one took credit for it, but it is widely suspected to be one of these strident, aggressive Underground members. Many people in the Underground are concerned that terrorism will spread throughout the country. It's our mission to prevent this from happening."

He paused, waiting for my response and to find out my interest in joining the mission.

"I think I'm here to help. God put me here for a reason," I said.

"I'm one of the leaders, so I can arrange it. We're going to meet with members of the Underground and refute the call to arms. We're going to speak. We're going to try to stop terrorism from spreading."

He was passionate and spoke with an air of confidence that we could do this.

"I've never spoken to an audience before."

"You're a natural, John. Just speak from your heart. You already know what to say. Just tell the people what you know. You can have a big impact. Many are losing their faith that God will create harmony and peace on Earth. They want to return to the cultural instincts of your era. They want to fight."

Anderson paused and went back to eating. I waited for him to continue talking, but he remained silent. I wondered if the milk in our cereal was powdered. I couldn't tell by the taste.

"You really think I can make a difference? That people will listen to what I have to say?" I asked.

"Yes," he said confidently.

"Okay, I'll do it," I said. "I think the Underground is on the right track. Your approach is absolutely the right one. If we learn to love ourselves, God, and our fellow man, there's no stopping us from regaining our freedom. God will honor our beliefs.

"For us to succeed, there must be a large number of people who are striving for peace. It's a matter of destiny. When enough people have the same intention, peace will be inevitable. It sounds like young souls are preventing freedom. They only care about power and ego. It's the young souls who are stirring up the terrorist activity. Our job is to limit their influence."

"I couldn't agree more," Anderson said.

"How much spiritual awareness is there among Americans?" I asked.

"You'd be surprised. It's not like in the 20th century. People have become spiritual. They began accepting the ideas you've talked about. The belief in oneness and that God loves everyone equally. These concepts are widely accepted now. I'll give you some material to read."

I nodded, accepting Anderson's offer.

"Oneness is widely accepted?" I asked. "I find that fascinating. That much spiritual awareness can only lead to a positive outcome. If you are right, then change must be near."

Chapter Two - The Underground

"Yes, it's almost time. I believe that you are a sign that we're nearing our destiny. You're here to set the events in motion."

"The prophecy?" I asked.

"Yes. God uses people to carry out his plans."

I looked at Anderson and reflected. "I always wanted to help God improve the world in some way. My goal has always been to help humanity transform into a spiritually aware civilization. To do that, I have strived to have a relationship with God and to feel God's presence in my life. Some people wanted families, some economic prosperity. I wanted to get closer to God. It's ironic for me to become one of God's messengers, because I used to tell people to be careful what they wish for. It might come true."

"That was your goal? To help humanity transform?" Anderson asked.

I nodded. "The planet needed help. It still does."

Anderson whistled softly. "Looks like your dream came true."

"It appears that way," I replied. "Although, I don't like to reflect on how my life is progressing. I prefer to live in the present moment, one day at a time, and not to focus on the past or dwell on the future. I try to leave the game plan to God and my higher self."

I paused. "Elan, a channeled soul that I've read, says that we should follow our passion. That's where we will find our life's path. In other words, don't get caught up in the external world. Instead, follow our internal passion and see where it leads. Forget about the past or the future. The key is to ground ourselves in the present moment and follow our passion.

"Said another way," I continued, "do what you love and say what you love and remain focused on that what you love. If you do that, then the universe will give you that outcome."

We were both silent for several seconds.

"You know," I said, "when I was riding here on that bus, I knew my destiny was being fulfilled. I could feel it. But my mind wasn't swimming with thoughts of fear like most of the people on that bus. We can't live like that and be close to God. The world isn't real anyway. It's just a stage. The only thing that is real on the physical plane is our soul. Everything else is an illusion."

"Are you aware of your soul?" Anderson asked.

I nodded. "I'm aware of my higher self, which I consider to be my soul. I can't prove it to you with words because it is something that you have to experience on your own.

"My higher self and I have ongoing communication. It's mostly guidance, where they tell me what to do, although sometimes they are playful and use quinky-dinks to get my attention. I also have guardian angels with me at all times. I even know some of their names, such as Joe, who is always with me.

"Then there's God, who hovers in the background, which is my connection to everything. I see God as a pervasive consciousness that's aware of every thought, and every action. God's in charge of the play. God's the director, and we are only the actors. Our role is to listen to the director, and not second-guess God's decisions. We do this by seeing the world as perfection, with only two outcomes, which are opportunities and blessings. Everything else is an illusion.

"So, all I need to do is stay in the present moment and follow my passion. Of course, being an enlightened old soul, I know how. I may have jumped three hundred

Chapter Two - The Underground

years into the future, but I still feel a close connection with God. The missing time doesn't matter; it's all just part of the master plan."

Anderson shook his head in wonder. "I've never met anyone like you before. You are consumed by spirituality."

"When we live by spiritual awareness, we want to talk about it," I said. "The more it's discussed, the closer we come to God. Spiritual interaction on the physical plane is one of the best ways for us to grow. It helps us to become even more aware."

After we finished our breakfast in the kitchen, we made our way to Anderson's office. He crossed the room to his desk and sat in his chair. Then he nodded for me to have a seat. He was wearing another freshly ironed printed shirt, freshly shaved, with his long hair carefully brushed. He was a handsome man.

Anderson removed a small box from a desk drawer and placed it on the desktop. "Inside this box is the history of the world since the early 1900s."

I raised my eyebrows in disbelief.

"They had DVDs in 1994, didn't they?" he asked, pushing the box toward me.

I opened it. Inside were about a dozen DVDs.

"No, we had CD-ROM. Each disk held about three hundred thousand pages of information."

"DVDs hold ten times that amount," Anderson said. "You can read them here at my desk on this computer screen or take the elevator down to the command center and use the wall monitor. I prefer the wall monitor, but you can use either one."

"Let's go downstairs," I said. "Those screens are huge."

We took the elevator down. Anderson told me that there were abstracts for various books and articles on each disk. It was a matter of switching back and forth between the abstracts and the complete book or article.

"I'll show you how," he said. "It's easy to use."

We exited the elevator and approached one of the large wall monitors. It was flush against the wall, approximately six feet square. We sat in two chairs backed up enough to see the screen clearly. On a stand next to his chair, Anderson picked up a device and showed it to me. "This controls the screen."

I looked at it. It was some type of computer touchpad.

"Let's start," he said. "Hand me the disk marked *1950-2000*."

I found the appropriate disk and handed it to him. He took the disk out of its case and inserted it into a computer on the floor beside his chair. He pressed on the touchpad, and the screen came to life.

He showed me how to use the touchpad. On the large screen was a menu of choices. There was an index of categories to choose from. The touchpad made it easy to make selections.

Anderson handed me the remote. "Here, take the control. Select the Economy category."

I did so by touching it. A listing of titles appeared, along with dates, author names, publications, and page lengths.

Anderson said, "The 1990s were about economic expansion and materialism. Except for a few regional wars, it was a period of stability. You can read about what you missed, but it doesn't get interesting until 1999 to 2001, that was when your economy began to decay and the terrorist wars began.

Chapter Two - The Underground

"If you have any problems, I'll be in the next room. I need to make a few calls. Have fun." He rose from his chair to leave.

"Phone calls?" I asked.

He laughed. "Wouldn't that be nice? No, I haven't talked on a phone in years. We use electronically scrambled communications. You know, computer to computer."

I nodded.

"You'll be helping me with my communications soon. They'll provide you with a current perspective on the Underground. Good reading." Anderson left the room.

I couldn't believe what I was reading. Whereas the last half of the 20th century had been relatively peaceful and economically stable, people weren't prepared for the first half of the 21st century. It was a time of war, disease, famine, social turmoil, natural disasters (floods, earthquakes, hurricanes), and economic crisis. Tens of millions of people died. It was a period of incomparable change. No one was unaffected by the events of that era. It was a period of change on a level never before imagined.

At the end of the first decade of the 21st century, America faltered economically and began to lose its position as the sole global superpower. After prolonged wars in the Middle East and Afghanistan, the economy began to falter. This led to an increase in social problems and the breakdown of government. People lost faith in government as the foundation of America. Society began to change in dramatic ways, leading to the breakup of the United States as states seceded and formed new countries.

One of the most interesting aspects of the changes was the rise of New Age thought and a turn away from organized religion. After the economy faltered, organized religion weakened noticeably. Fewer people went to church, and more people sought spirituality using metaphysical concepts. They sought spiritual answers to the problems that plagued the world. Many began openly questioning the Bible as the only source of spiritual knowledge. Many believed that organized religions and outdated beliefs did not provide the answers to their problems. New Age metaphysical beliefs became the new vogue, and a transition toward New Age thought was trending.

"How's it going?" Anderson asked.

I turned toward the door and saw him coming into the room. "Good. How long have I been reading?"

"About six hours. Are you hungry?"

"Sure. Should I turn off the screen?"

"No, the computer will power down automatically once you stop. When you come back and turn it on, it will remember where you left off."

I nodded.

We walked to the elevator. The door closed, and we started up. I looked at Anderson. "Does Christianity exist today? Are there any churches?"

"No. The world steadily turned Gnostic after the churches dissolved. There are no more churches. Today, everyone has their own spirituality. People recognize that Gnostic spirituality – knowing God from within – is the true source of spiritual awareness."

The elevator door opened, and we stepped out into the kitchen area. Anderson's assistant had prepared our lunch. On the table were tuna sandwiches, potato chips, and milk.

Anderson ate some chips and smiled. "In your time, potato chips weren't healthy because of the high fat content

Chapter Two - The Underground

and lack of vitamins. Today, with the help of scientists, potato chips provide excellent nutrition."

"That's true," I replied. "I avoided chips for that reason. They were considered junk food. Looking back, the food industry was pathetic. There was so little nutritional value in so many products. It's surprising anyone was healthy."

Anderson changed the subject. "I talked today with a leader from the Chicago area: Henderson. He's interested in you. He wants us to come to Chicago as soon as possible. We can begin there."

I nodded, relieved that we were leaving the prison.

"You're going to be the attraction. You'll give lectures to a small group of selected Underground members. Henderson will tell people that you are the fulfillment of the prophecy, and that you were recently cryogenically unfrozen. We considered obscuring your identity, but it's better to tell the truth."

"What will I talk about?" I asked.

"What you have told me. Just speak from your heart about what you know. You could prepare a speech, but I don't think it's necessary. You already know what to say."

"Does it concern you that I'm nervous or that I might not do a good job?"

He shook his head. "You'll do a good job. It's your destiny."

I hoped he was right.

"By the way, have you read about the earth shift yet?" Anderson asked.

"Not yet, although I read yesterday that they had to move the financial center from New York to Omaha because of flooding."

"A book by David Morton is excellent. Read it after lunch, and we'll talk about it tonight."

I nodded and took a bite. The sandwich was good.

"Andy, where do you get your electricity?"

"A hydrogen fuel cell. You didn't have them yet in 1994.

* * * * *

I began reading about the earth shift and earth changes. Throughout the early 21st century, the weather was treacherous: powerful storms brought tremendous floods, droughts, heat waves, cold waves, windstorms, and hurricanes. The unusual became the norm. When the weatherman warned of strange weather, no longer did people ignore the warning. Everyone wondered when the next record-breaking storm would hit.

Strong earthquakes and volcanic eruptions accompanied the strange weather. These weather anomalies and earth changes led to something profound. In 2037, the earth shifted. In a matter of hours, continents moved and broke up. Where once there was land, there was now water; where once there was water, there was now land. The map of the world was instantly changed.

The United States lost a third of its land mass to water inundation, mostly in the West. More than a quarter of the population perished. It was the same worldwide. All of the continents radically transformed. The world would never be the same.

"How's it coming?" Anderson asked, coming back into the room.

I turned and saw him standing behind me. "I can't believe what I just read. It's so incredible."

Chapter Two – The Underground

"Let's go have some dinner."

I put down the touchpad and rose from my chair. We made our way to the elevator.

Waiting for us in the kitchen was pasta in a red sauce, green beans, and watermelon. Anderson ate like this, while the rest of the prison population ate Dry food. It was a stunning contrast. I had a pang of guilt knowing what was going on around us and felt a bit uncomfortable. I also realized that Anderson could not help the Underground if he was dead.

We sat down and began our meal.

"John, how come the New Age movement was not more popular during your time?"

I finished chewing the delicious pasta. "Christianity had a stranglehold over people's beliefs. Very few were open to questioning their beliefs. Such as whether Jesus was God's son, or that God in Heaven determined their fate. Moreover, the metaphysical ideas of New Agers were considered a taboo area. Something was needed to get people to reconsider Gnostic ideas of oneness and reincarnation as the true reality.

"It's amazing that Christianity lasted as long as it did," I said. "It had so many false foundations: a patriarchy that neglected the equality of women; the belief in separateness from God; Jesus as God's son; Jesus as Savior; God determining our fate based on morality; our salvation dependent on our belief in Jesus. All of these were false.

"Let's look at the belief in separation from God. This led to the belief that each person is separate from one another, and uniquely blessed by the grace of God. Thus, the millionaire was blessed by the grace of God, while the homeless person was not. Such was the mantra of the 20th century. If one person was fortunate, then God favored him or her. If another was not favored, then God did not bless them. And so on.

"The belief in separateness was at the heart of American life in the 20th century. It was quite common to judge people for their achievements and failures. People were so used to judging others by their deeds and achievements that accepting people for simply being human would require a whole new way of thinking. A judgmental Christian God would no longer fit this new mindset of oneness."

I reached for another piece of watermelon.

"Can you give me some specific examples in the 1990s that showed this belief in separation?" Anderson asked.

"The homeless problem. America was an affluent society, but we did little to alleviate the problem of homelessness. As a group, we denied that the problem existed. Every year we spent hundreds of billions of dollars on national defense, but practically nothing on the homeless.

"Our competitive lifestyle is another example. We all competed to see who could have the nicest house. It started in kindergarten with our first report card and continued with our first job review. The homeless were considered losers in America's dog-eat-dog world of competition. To the winners go the spoils.

"This led to the neglect of education so that the affluent could maintain their dominance. The lower classes received a negligible education, and nobody screamed for equity in education. We loved to talk about equality, but equality among school districts was nonexistent. Most school districts relied on property taxes for financing. This led to a class-based society and maintained the status quo. The large inner cities literally shoved kids through the

Chapter Two - The Underground

school system, even if that meant children didn't learn how to read and write. It was a disgrace."

Anderson interrupted. "John, it sounds like America faltered because it lacked spiritual awareness."

I nodded. "That's obvious. America reflected society's values. As the scripture says: *By their fruits, you shall know them.* As a society, we made poor decisions. A spiritual society would have remedied these problems. Instead, equality was systematically denied to the deprived segments of society. We lacked compassion. It was selfishness on a societal scale.

"God represents the whole, and all are part of the whole," I continued. "When there is someone in the group who needs help, we must come to their aid. Equality becomes the standard because we are all equal. America, in the late 20th century, was ignoring equality."

Anderson nodded.

We ate in silence.

"Our trip has been scheduled," he said.

I looked up in surprise. "When do we leave?"

"Two weeks. And if everything goes well in Chicago, we'll travel to other cities."

"Is this going to be dangerous?" I asked.

Anderson smiled. "Are you afraid?"

"I just want to know what we're up against."

"Our trip is approved by the Underground Council. We'll have escorts and security. Everything should be fine. We'll still have to be careful, though. We don't want any contact with the Chinese."

He paused. "I think there are forces bigger than us in charge of our mission. I think your destiny will be fulfilled."

Chapter Three

Leaving the Prison

The time passed quickly. Day after day, I rose early and took the elevator down to the command center, where I sat transfixed, reading about this future civilization I had never imagined. I occasionally talked with Anderson, but he was busy preparing for our trip.

In the early 21st century, after the U.S. economy stopped growing, people wanted the government to take care of them. Interest groups competed against each other. Everyone wanted help. Groups faced off against each other, refusing to give ground. Wall Street bankers wanted bailouts for their bad decisions and greed, unions and government workers wanted job security.

Instead of following their hearts, people followed their self-interests. Instead of focusing on humanity, they focused on their quality of life. People became antagonistic towards each other. Politicians had to decide which groups to help. It was a mess.

One group actually welcomed the changes. These were the New Agers. Initially, they were outside the mainstream, and few people even knew they existed. The little press they did receive was negative and mocking, and their only avenues of spreading knowledge were books, seminars, weekend expositions in major cities, word-of-mouth, and the Internet.

The New Age movement was relegated to the fringe. People were so detached from metaphysics that, even after problems began, New Agers remained a small group for several years. Most people weren't exposed to metaphysics, and only a small percentage of people knew the concept of oneness. The rest believed in separation, and the duality of good and evil.

This steadily changed after the economy faltered and stopped growing. More and more people exposed themselves to and accepted metaphysical concepts. This amazing change generated a profound sense of hope throughout the country.

* * * * *

Finally, the two weeks passed. I woke one morning to voices in a distant room. I dressed and went to see our visitor. When I arrived in Anderson's office, Jackson was seated in a chair next to Anderson. I wondered if his presence was related to our trip. It was near the time for us to leave.

"Hello, Johnson," Jackson said.

I nodded to him. He wore a scraggly beard and thick mustache. I noticed how dirty and worn his clothes were, and wondered if they were like that on our first encounter.

"John, please have a seat," Anderson said.

I did as Anderson instructed.

"We're leaving tonight. Jackson and his friends will be here around midnight. This is short notice, but San Antonio is an isolated prison, and we have only so many opportunities. A driver can pick us up tonight. Otherwise, it could be another week."

"I'm ready," I said.

Chapter Three - Leaving the Prison

"The walk to the wall will take two hours. Jackson and his friends will make sure that the journey is uneventful. We must be careful because other groups inside the prison can be dangerous. But not to worry, Jackson's men are very good.

"After we reach the wall, there's an opening to a tunnel. Inside the tunnel is a light-rail system with a metal track for a small wagon. The wagon has an electric motor and travels five miles per hour. It holds one man comfortably. The tunnel was built for me years ago by the Underground. It's used to bring in my supplies.

"The security system of the prison is designed to watch the outside; they don't care about the inside. They use infrared cameras to ensure outside security. A camera is located every half-mile on top of the wall. The security system does have one weakness, which is a long tunnel. The cameras are only good for about one hundred yards. After that, there is no security. The tunnel is one hundred fifty yards long. We've never had any problems with it.

"Once we get on the outside, a truck will pick us up. We'll take the truck to Arkansas. It will be a government-marked truck, and I foresee no problems. The driver will be Chinese and a government worker. In addition, he'll have papers that authorize him to drive to Arkansas ..."

I interrupted. "We have help from the Chinese? Are they part of the Underground?"

He nodded. "Yes, we have many Chinese friends. If it wasn't for them, we couldn't travel. They risk their lives for our freedom. But then, they understand that all of life is one integrated consciousness, and that we are all *one*. Everyone in the world has been exposed to this truth, to some degree. Metaphysics is as common today as the Bible was in the 20th century."

Anderson leaned back in his chair and looked at me. "That's it. Any questions?"

I shook my head.

Jackson rose from his chair. "I'll see you guys tonight." He turned and left the room.

Anderson turned to me, "Have you read Nostradamus' description of the next civilization?"

"No," I replied eagerly.

"It's on the DVD labeled the *Tomorrow File*. Read it before we leave."

"Okay."

I placed the DVD in the computer slot and pressed the remote. The screen came on, and I quickly found the material Anderson had suggested.

So, this was what it would be like at some point in the future. A complete reversal from materialism, selfishness, greed, power, and racism. No longer did people judge each other or compete against each other. People were concerned with sustainability and living in harmony with nature and their fellow human beings.

Spiritually, nearly everyone was enlightened. They knew that every individual had a different spiritual journey. Whereas one person might be a scientist and another a teacher, each was a spiritual equal. People recognized the oneness and equality in everything.

Also, there were few cultural distinctions between the sexes. For the first time, equality between the sexes was a reality. People coexisted in a realm of love. People understood they were God, and this made it easy to love each other.

Children were brought up to understand that they were manifestations of God, as was nature. They were taught that it was their responsibility to act as a

Chapter Three - Leaving the Prison

manifestation of God and to treat the planet with respect. Children also were taught that this life is one life in a series of incarnations, and that we are here to nurture and develop our soul. They were taught to listen to their inner voice for guidance, and that spirituality comes from within. And that each person has his or her own unique spirituality and beliefs.

Love flourished on the planet, an incredible love and joy that was never experienced by my generation. It occurred because people accepted themselves as God. They viewed everything in interrelated terms, focusing on the whole.

Each person was given reign to make his or her own decisions. This freedom was only limited by one of God's universal laws: thou shall not force your will upon another. People realized that eternal souls do not need government to meddle in their lives.

However, this did not preclude people from helping others. The key was to know when to help, and when to stay out of the way. This future generation trusted their intuition and knew how to listen to their heart. They used inner guidance to maintain harmony and not allow problems to escalate.

"Are you ready, John?" Anderson asked, coming back into the room.

"Sure." I pressed the remote, and the screen went black.

"Take the DVDs with you. There'll be computers where we travel."

I picked up the box of DVDs, and we walked to the elevator.

"Jackson's here. It's time to leave."

I nodded. "Are we coming back after the trip?"

"I am. I don't know your fate. Maybe you'll return with me, maybe not."

The elevator opened. Jackson stood waiting for us in shorts, a short-sleeved shirt, and army-issue lace-up boots. He looked like a tour guide.

"This sector is empty tonight," he said. "My men are strung out in a path leading to the wall. Let's get going while it's safe."

"Let's go," Anderson said.

At the door leading to the outside, Anderson's assistant was waiting for us with two backpacks. We put them on. Anderson said goodbye to Peterson and told him not to open the door for anyone until he returned.

The massive steel door opened, and we headed out into the hot August night. Jackson mumbled something into his handset, then turned to us. "We're in a cocoon of about 20 men. Once we're out of this sector, it's a clear break to the wall. Follow me."

After a while, our eyes adjusted to the darkness, and we could see more clearly. From time to time, we noticed Jackson's men. They would suddenly slip out of a building entrance and then take up positions behind us.

We walked through an empty, desolate area that at one time was a business district. There were no signs of life now. No sounds, no lights, no evidence of recent habitation. It seemed like Anderson didn't have any neighbors. If this was what they called a sector, it was empty.

Soon we were outside the old business district and on the outskirts of the city. By now, we could see most of Jackson's men. They had formed a gauntlet, with their backs to the old business district from which we had just

Chapter Three - Leaving the Prison

departed. From their body language, I realized that they weren't coming with us to the wall.

Jackson stopped. "There's nothing between here and the wall. Nothing but empty desert. There's no reason for us to come with you. I'll send Olson to show you the entrance to the tunnel and help you with the wagon."

Olson stepped forward. I recognized him from our earlier meeting. His same expressionless face looked at Anderson and me without saying a word.

"When can I expect you back, Andy?" Jackson asked.

Anderson responded, "I'm not sure. The Underground will send in a man when a date has been determined. You'll be told the date and time when I'll be returning."

Jackson nodded. "Very good. I'll see you when you get back."

Jackson turned and walked toward his men.

Without saying a word, Olson started walking toward the wall. Anderson and I followed. Luckily, the moon was bright; otherwise, we would have stumbled through the brush that littered the landscape.

It was a hot night. My sweaty shirt stuck to my body, and I could feel the heat from the dirt through my shoes. The terrain was relatively flat, and we walked in nearly a straight line. After the first mile, we looked back. San Antonio loomed behind us in the moonlight. There were no lights from the lack of power, but there were an array of small fires scattered across the horizon.

After more than an hour of nonstop walking, we finally reached the base of the huge wall. The tunnel entrance was covered by a camouflaged tarp. Olson removed the tarp, under which rested a wagon perched on tiny metal tracks. "Press the switch, and it will go all the way to the end," he said, his first words to me.

"John, you go first," Anderson said.

I got down into the wagon. The tunnel was about six feet high by six feet wide. There was no light. It was pitch black. "Olson, what do I do when I get to the other end?" I asked.

In a voice devoid of emotion, Olson answered. "It will stop on its own. Remove the tarp and toggle the switch."

"Roger that," I said. "See you in a few, Andy." I toggled the switch.

Instantly, the wagon lurched forward, and the electric motor hummed to life. A small light on the front of the wagon blinked on and off, and I could see 10 to 20 feet ahead of me as the wagon rambled forward. It was a smooth ride. About a minute later, the engine turned off, and the wagon coasted to a stop.

I reached up and removed the overhead tarp, then climbed out of the wagon. Glancing back at the prison, I saw the huge wall, which was indelibly stamped into my memory. I reached back down to the wagon and flipped the switch. It instantly lurched into reverse.

I sat on the tarp and waited for Anderson. In the distance, just a quarter mile away, one of the towers between the wall and me was armed with weapons that would prevent a mass exodus. But I assumed I was safe here.

It was quiet in the desert and smelled of dirt and brush. The night sky was clear, with bright stars and a full moon. I found the North Star and Orion. After a few minutes of searching, I saw Mars over the horizon. Its red hue was barely discernible. It was reassuring to see the familiar sky.

I heard the wagon come to a stop. Anderson's head popped out of the tunnel. He smiled. "Let's go to Chicago."

Chapter Three - Leaving the Prison

We carefully placed the tarp back over the tunnel entrance and started walking across the desert. According to Jackson, if we walked in a straight line away from the prison, eventually we would come to a paved road. We were to wait at that road until we were picked up.

As we walked, we dodged the brush and maintained our direction by following the distant mountains. The ground was flat and hard, and the night was muggy and humid. The walk took a lot out of us. We stopped occasionally to get a drink of water from our backpacks. Our mood was subdued by the danger that lurked – escaped prisoners were executed – yet we were both confident we would get to Chicago. We were on a mission.

"I see a road," I said.

We walked closer and found a place to sit. It was still dark, and we had to wait until sunrise for the truck to pick us up. We each had a light blanket in our backpack. We sat on our blankets and talked.

"Were you affected by some of the things you read?" Anderson asked.

"Sure, how could I not be? I'm still in shock after reading about the end of my old civilization. I'm amazed at the massive changes that have occurred. It's hard to imagine that California is now a series of islands."

We talked for more than an hour in the moonlight, staring at the stars and smelling the fragrance of the desert. Anderson wanted to hear about the 20th century, and I wanted to hear more about the 23rd century and the Underground. We each kept trying to change the subject. Our conversation switched back and forth between eras. We hardly noticed the faint light of daybreak.

"Tell me about Jesus?" Anderson asked.

"Jesus was an advanced soul," I said. "We are too, but he was much more evolved than us. He came to Earth to show us what is possible. He came as an example to plant seeds for our spiritual evolution. Most of the information in the Bible about Jesus is correct, and some information was withheld. For instance, the impact of the Essenes on his life and what they taught him."

Anderson looked at me with keen interest.

"Do you know about the Essenes?" I asked.

"Not very much," he replied.

"The Essenes were a secret Gnostic society, descended from the survivors of Atlantis. Atlantis was an advanced civilization that ended in destruction about ten thousand years before Jesus. The Essenes saved spiritual knowledge from the Atlantean civilization by passing it down for generations. The Essenes were a special group. They were studying much of what Jesus taught and were his teachers. Their mission was to prevent what had happened to Atlantis from happening again. They wanted to preserve the spiritual knowledge of that era and create peace on Earth.

"The Essenes lived apart from society in small communes, located in various places throughout Europe. There were many of these communes, and the Essenes traveled back and forth and communicated with each other. The main commune was at Qumran, near the Dead Sea. This is where the famous Dead Sea scrolls were found. However, Jesus attended the commune at Mount Carmel, which was nearby Qumran. It was there that his mother, Mary, and grandmother, Anna, lived.

"Each commune, essentially, was a school, and the Essenes revered knowledge. Children, both male and female, were taught a rigorous education when they

Chapter Three - Leaving the Prison

were young: subjects such as the Torah, mathematics, astronomy, and something called the mysteries, which included metaphysics. They were teaching metaphysics to children two thousand years before I was born. My generation didn't even know what the word metaphysics meant. The spiritual knowledge of Atlantis was largely lost to us, even though the Essenes tried to pass it on.

"The Essenes were keepers of knowledge. They collected knowledge on journeys and passed it on to generations. Their purpose was to bring peace to humankind. It's hard to explain the extensive knowledge they had. For instance, they knew when Jesus was going to be born. They also knew who his mother would be. In fact, they knew Jesus' entire life story before he was even born. They were already prepared, waiting to teach him.

"Mount Carmel is where Jesus was educated. This truth was kept secret by the Catholic Church. It wasn't revealed because of what the Essenes believed and taught. They were Gnostics and believed in a direct link from their soul to God. The Church destroyed and covered up all information regarding the Essenes, their beliefs, and teachings. This cover-up prevented Gnostic beliefs from having an impact on society.

"The Essenes knew the meaning of life. Interestingly, Jesus knew this knowledge intuitively at a young age. He was aware that *all* is God. He was very aware as a child. As a boy, he never argued or became upset. He spoke with a clear, beautiful voice, and simply stated facts or parables. Even at a young age, he could explain to people, in clear terms, the meaning of life …

Anderson interrupted. "How interesting. Jesus was born at the ideal time in the ideal place. Mount Carmel was a school that allowed him to blossom into a spiritual master. No wonder he was such a great teacher. He was taught by masters. Tell me more. What did the Essenes know? And what did the previous culture of Atlantis understand?"

"The concepts of reincarnation and oneness with God, and that we are a combination of lives spent, each life adding to our soul's maturity. Jesus had developed his soul to near perfection. In fact, his soul was too advanced to learn many new lessons here on Earth, but he volunteered to come. He came to show us, to be an example. He came to spark our spiritual evolution and to begin the ascent into the Age of Aquarius.

"Jesus was like all of us, another spark of God. His distinction was his spiritual awareness. Even as a young boy, he was already enlightened. He understood that he wasn't separate from God. He had an advantage that we don't: he knew it wasn't his first life and that he was an evolved soul. He knew that he had lived many previous lifetimes, and that his spirituality had evolved from these experiences. He understood that everyone else would live many more lives and evolve spiritually just like himself.

"The entire message that Jesus brought isn't in the Bible. He spoke about reincarnation and oneness. However, the people weren't ready to grasp these concepts when the New Testaments were compiled. They preferred to believe that God was separate from them and to be feared. They weren't ready to believe that they were God. The concept of oneness was too big for that era. It implied that everyone was equal, and that idea was too radical 2,300 years ago. Subsequently, these two concepts were left out of the Bible."

"I don't know much about the Bible," Anderson said. "Bibles weren't read much after your generation. After the

Chapter Three - Leaving the Prison

churches withered, so did the Bible. The Bible has been considered archaic for many generations. There's been no need for me to study it, or even the significance of Jesus' life. Tell me more. I think his life is more important than I thought."

"Oh, yes, his life was very significant," I said. "If it wasn't for Jesus, the New Age movement during my lifetime wouldn't have occurred, and the spirituality espoused today wouldn't exist. Jesus was the savior of the world, and the Essenes knew this. They also knew he wouldn't be easily accepted by their generation. They knew his message was too advanced. They hoped one day, in the far future, people would read their scrolls and grasp the meaning of life.

"It's interesting how the Essenes lived and what they believed. They accepted equality of the sexes. Many of the Essene teachers were women. In fact, when Jesus sent his disciples to preach to the world, he sent them in pairs of men and women. He did this because there were so many women among his followers.

"The Essenes also believed in unconditional love and sharing. In their communes, nobody used money. Everything was shared. People loved one another without condition. There was no sense of rivalry among commune members. They already accepted the message that Jesus preached to the world: Peace and goodwill toward others.

"The Essenes also believed in meditation. They taught their children to begin meditating at the age of four or five, to get in touch with their inner spirit. They believed that spirituality is individual, and that meditation is the best way to nurture our spirit.

"Going to the temple (to church) was not mandatory. Even though everyone was taught the Torah, the Essenes believed that, when one understands the meaning of life, going to a temple isn't necessary."

"Wow," Anderson interjected, "it's interesting how we've accepted that belief today. Gnostic beliefs and a hierarchical church are conflicting concepts. No wonder Gnostic beliefs were suppressed during your lifetime." He laughed. "Can you imagine being in one of those communes 2,300 years ago and realizing that it would be centuries before society became enlightened? How depressing!"

I nodded smiling. "It's also interesting what the Essenes did *not* believe in: war and violence. They learned from their ancestors that war and violence never solve any problems. In fact, the only way one could get kicked out of an Essene commune was to display violence. It wasn't tolerated.

"Their faith was incredible," I continued. "When the Romans raided the Qumran commune in 68 A.D., they tortured the Essenes to reveal the locations of their hidden knowledge. The Essenes wouldn't say a word. They stowed away their knowledge in caves and refused to reveal its locations."

I paused and looked at the rising sun. We'd been so engrossed in talking about the Essenes that we'd missed the sunrise.

"What else did they believe?" Anderson asked, wanting to learn as much as he could.

"The Golden Rule is the paramount law: Thou shall love *all* unconditionally. The Essenes believed that this law takes precedence and leaves the rest as supporting guidelines. They also taught that we create our own reality by our thoughts and beliefs, and that it is important to direct our intent to what we want. This is called

Chapter Three - Leaving the Prison

manifesting, the same as the New Age movement taught in the 20th century."

"And they taught all of this to Jesus?" Anderson asked.

"Well, to set the record straight, when they taught Jesus, he was called Yeshua. The name Jesus was first used in Germany in 1632, when they translated the Bible into German. It was said that, if you knew him, you would love him. He was generally quiet, but if you mentioned God and spiritual subjects, he quickly came to life. He was intense and adamant about sharing God with others. He loved to talk about God, and he believed that we must share God in our everyday existence.

"He spoke softly and was at peace with himself. According to the Essenes, he exemplified goodness, compassion, and an understanding of God. The Essenes considered these traits to be the treasure that we take with us to heaven."

"It sounds like how we treat other people is more important than achievement," Anderson said.

"How we treat other people *is* our achievement," I answered.

"Did the Essenes consider Jesus the Messiah?"

"Probably more a messenger than a messiah. Jesus himself, never claimed to be the Messiah. He called himself the son of man, and he knew that we are all children of God. He knew that all souls are essentially the same, although not all of us have the same spiritual development. It takes many lessons to reach Jesus' level of advancement.

"According to the Essenes, the biggest misconception in the Bible is that Jesus died for our sins. This implies that we are judged for our misdeeds. That is false. The only person who judges us is ourselves.

"Jesus' message was misinterpreted. He said that we are all children of God. He was trying to say that we are all eternal. In his time, this idea was too difficult for people to understand, and information was suppressed.

"Jesus is to be marveled, not worshipped, because we are his equals. He was an example of what is possible. If we accept him as a worthy messenger, then we can find the right path. That's why Jesus said, 'No man shall come to the Father except by me.' He was spiritually ahead of us. Our goal is to find the path that he found."

Anderson was silent for a long time. "Where did you learn about the Essenes?"

"Several books. In one of them, Jesus' life was revealed to Dolores Cannon during a hypnotic regression by someone who had been an Essene at Qumran in a past life. In another, Jesus' life was revealed to an author named Claire Heartsong using channeling."

Anderson looked at me with a mischievous grin and said, "I'm not surprised. It had to be a supernatural source."

"During my lifetime, this information was revealed to the public with little notice. Most people dismissed it as esoteric, or crazy nonsense."

Anderson rose and walked around, kicking the dirt. This was the most emotion he'd displayed since we met. "I've always thought that Jesus was like us. My God, we are finishing what Jesus started!"

"You could look at it that way."

Chapter Four

Chicago

Shortly after sunrise, we saw a cloud of dust in the distance. As the cloud drew nearer, I sensed Anderson's apprehension. He hadn't been outside the prison in 30 years.

The truck slowed to a stop. It was similar to a 20th-century eighteen-wheeler, although taller and not as wide. The Chinese driver got out of the truck and strode to the back of the trailer. He wore a bright yellow jumpsuit with Chinese letters stenciled across his chest. We met him at the rear of the trailer. He glanced at us as he unlatched the swinging doors, then nodded for us to climb inside.

Anderson climbed in, and I followed. It was dark inside and smelled of cardboardr from the boxes that filled the front half of the trailer. The floor was wood, the walls and ceiling aluminum. There were no windows.

The driver reached into a shirt pocket and produced a piece of paper. Anderson accepted the note. Then the swinging doors slammed shut, and the latch locked.

It was pitch black, except for a tiny bit of light coming through a small open hatch in one of the rear doors. Anderson stayed close to the hatch and read the note.

"It's from Stevenson in Arkansas, another leader in the Underground. This truck will stop in Fayetteville tonight. He'll be waiting for us. We should be there before dark."

Our eyes slowly adjusted to the dark. After a few minutes, Anderson and I could see each other clearly. I removed my backpack and stretched out on the hard wooden floor, using the backpack for a pillow. Before long, I fell asleep.

My last glimpse was of Anderson, sitting up against the inside aluminum wall, deep in thought. No doubt still wondering what Jesus and his life meant to our trip.

* * * * *

Sometime later, the truck jerked to a stop. I opened my eyes and remembered where I was. My eyes slowly adjusted to the darkness as I looked toward Anderson.

"I was wondering if you were going to wake up," he said.

I sat up and stretched, and my senses came to life. "How long was I asleep?"

Before he could answer, the trailer doors unlatched and swung open, filling the trailer with light. The Chinese driver had a blank expression and didn't say a word.

We carefully climbed out of the trailer. As my feet hit the ground, I looked at the surrounding area. It was an expanse of rolling hills, oak trees, brush, and dry tall grass. The afternoon sun was hot and low in the western sky. The high humidity made the heat nearly unbearable. I winced from the discomfort.

The truck was parked off the highway. We were out in the country, away from any buildings or people. It appeared that we hadn't reached our destination yet because nobody was here to meet us.

We waited as the Chinese driver closed and locked the trailer door. Without expression, he turned and faced us.

Chapter Four – Chicago

"What do we do?" Anderson asked him.

"Wait, wait," he said in a staccato manner.

"How long?"

"Wait, wait," the driver repeated, then turned and walked to the truck cabin. The engine roared to life, and we watched as he drove off.

Anderson and I stood in silence. Finally, he turned to me. "I suppose we wait here. Maybe he dropped us at a precise location. Let's get off the highway and keep our heads down."

There were no distinguishable features to our location. I didn't know how anyone was going to find us. I followed Anderson, and we sat a few yards off the road and waited.

"I couldn't sleep in the truck," Anderson said. "I was thinking about Jesus and the Essenes. It's energizing when you discover knowledge. It's like getting a shot of adrenaline."

I nodded. "I remember when I learned about Jesus. I was searching for answers, and I somehow knew his life was a big piece of the puzzle. When I asked for knowledge about his life, I was given answers. Knowledge started coming in waves. In a short period, I was exposed to more knowledge than I ever dreamed possible …"

"I hear a car," Anderson interrupted.

As the car came closer, it slowed, then stopped parallel to us.

"Well, let's go see who it is," Anderson said. "Obviously, they knew where to look."

The old beat-up car appeared to be made of plastic. It was shaped something like a Toyota van, with windows everywhere and a huge windshield.

The driver got out to meet us. His red silk jumpsuit looked like a lightweight astronaut uniform. He was

Anderson's age, a handsome man with blue eyes and short, curly blonde hair.

He met us with a big, energetic smile. "Hello, Andy." They shook hands. "It's good to see you again."

"Stevenson, this is John."

Stevenson put out his hand to greet me. "John, it's a pleasure to meet you. I've been talking with others about your trip with Anderson. I'm excited. I think a lot of good will come from it."

"One question," I said, shaking Stevenson's hand. "How did you find us?"

"I was on top of that hill with binoculars." He pointed off in the distance. "When you passed the last town, I was radioed. I've been waiting here since noon. Let's get off the road." He motioned for us to get in the car, and we were quickly on our way.

"I can't believe I'm in the same car with you, John," Stevenson said, as he drove.

"Why is that?" I asked from the back seat.

"You're the sign we've been waiting for. Soon, word will get around that you're here. The result will be a change of heart, which will stifle the urge towards violence. We've been expecting peace and freedom the world over. You're here to help. I, for one, have been waiting for many years. Even if it takes hundreds of years to attain peace and harmony, it's worth the wait. Knowing that you exist is uplifting. It implies that we're getting close."

"Where are we going?" Anderson asked, seated in the front passenger seat.

"My house. You'll stay with me tonight. Tomorrow morning, I'll take you to the airport, where you'll fly to Chicago." He pointed straight ahead. "We're almost to town. I live over there."

Chapter Four - Chicago

We approached the city near dusk. It was a relatively large city, with a skyline and suburbs as far as I could see. The population must have been over a million. After reading about repressive conditions in Omaha, I wondered how free these people here were. I remembered that the Chinese government controlled everything.

"Is it dangerous for us to be driving through here?" I asked.

Stevenson glanced at me in the mirror. "No. We're passive here, and the Chinese allow us some freedom. Over the years, we've proven that we will obey their laws, so they give us room to breathe. The one freedom that we cherish is the ability to move around the city. As long as we don't start any problems, they allow it. We have a unique city, and many would like to live here. That's impossible, of course, because the Chinese allow no migration."

I remembered reading about the no-migration policy. The Chinese tracked the population with computers. If anyone acted suspiciously, they were quickly interrogated and possibly sent to one of the prisons. Freedom was vicarious and limited throughout the country. It was a totalitarian state taken to the extreme.

As we entered the city, I was startled by its resemblance to the past; the architecture was similar to the 20th century. I'd expected something different. The streets were clean, though haggard and worn. Everything appeared aged and in need of renewal. It reminded me of the comparison I used to make between the United States and other countries. America had always been the most modern, with third-world countries a few steps behind.

Fayetteville was several steps behind. Stevenson's tattered neighborhood should have been torn down a hundred years ago. The Chinese had given the residents the option to stay or move into government apartments. Many had chosen to stay. It was an eerie place, dark and decrepit.

As we drove into Stevenson's driveway, he told us to be silent as we entered the house. He led us through the front door. The inside matched the outside. Everything was old and worn out.

He led us to a back bedroom, where he removed a ragged piece of carpet that revealed a trap door. He reached down, opened it, and walked down the stairs into the darkness. Anderson and I followed.

A faint light glowed within. As we reached the bottom, I could see the outline of the room, but darkness obscured the details. Stevenson lived here. The clean and dry smell revealed that. It wasn't dank, like most basements. This was his living quarters. He spent a great deal of time down here.

Stevenson hit a switch to turn on the lights, and I almost gasped as the future hit me square in the face. I looked around in amazement. The modern amenities were even more impressive than Anderson's. Electronics completely filled one wall. Monitors and wall screens on another, and an array of computers on yet another. Communications equipment packed the large, 200-square-foot room. The contrast with the main floor was amazing. No one entering the main entrance would expect to find this in the basement.

Anderson was also impressed. He slowly studied the room with a keen sense of interest.

Stevenson approached a printout and began reading it. Anderson stalked the room, staring at this and that. I watched both of them. This was an unusual situation. It must have been rare for Stevenson to allow anyone into

Chapter Four - Chicago

this room. He had taken a risk, a huge risk if we were captured and talked.

"We have an hour or two," he said. "Then both of you need to get some sleep. The plane to Chicago leaves at dawn, and I want to be early. I wish I could go with you to Chicago, but the Underground didn't want to take the risk. It's the right decision."

I looked at Stevenson closely. His sculpted features and intense, piercing blue eyes were a facade. He was a sensitive, emotional man. I sensed sadness and softness beneath his keen intellect. He was honest, and it showed. I wanted to ask if he had any family and friends, but I suspected his answers would bring sadness and pain.

"John," he said, "I have some photos of the early 21st century, even some from the late 20th century. Do you want to see them?"

I was excited. "Sure, I would love to."

He walked to a cabinet and fumbled inside for a DVD. Then he motioned for Anderson and me to grab folding chairs from against the wall. "We'll use the large screen," he said.

As we seated ourselves, Stevenson pressed a few buttons, and the screen came to life.

"Have you seen the new geography of the planet since your time?" Stevenson asked.

"Only from what I've read," I replied.

A view of the United States from space appeared. I could clearly see the water inundation and massive changes to the continent.

I whistled. "It's amazing how the continents have changed. Wow, look at how the Great Lakes emptied into the Mississippi River has formed an inland sea, splitting the country in two."

Stevenson pressed the remote, and the next picture appeared.

"The photos are incredibly clear, almost realistic," I said. "When was this technology invented?"

"It's three-dimensional digital photography," Stevenson said. "I think it was the 21st century. These photos are one hundred megapixels."

"Impressive," I said. "We didn't have this technology during the 20th century. I suppose the photos can be edited and touched up?"

"Oh, sure. Digital is easy to work with," Stevenson said. "We have software today that can do nearly anything to a picture. You can take several different photographs and combine them and not be able to tell they were combined."

"What's this picture?" I asked.

"Israel in 2027. As you can see, it was nearly destroyed." Stevenson pressed a few buttons and displayed several more pictures of what was once Israel.

"This is the aftermath of nuclear weapons?" I asked.

"Yes, it was bombed by terrorists. As you can see, not much survived."

Stevenson clicked the remote.

"These are from the Asian famines from the 21st century. Tens of millions of people starved. Millions of people would congregate at sources of food, but there was never enough."

"These photos remind me of the famines in Africa in the late 1980s," I said.

"People should have realized then," Anderson said, "that those famines signaled famines for everyone. Famines were forecast by people like Nostradamus and the prophets in *Revelation*. The famines in your lifetime

Chapter Four - Chicago

were the symbol of the devastation to come. Those famines were a sign from God that it was time to change, or else there would be hell to pay."

"I agree," I said. "I saw those famines as a sign, and I recognized what they symbolized. At the time, however, only a small portion of the population was spiritually aware. When the signs came, it was nearly impossible for people to heed these warnings."

Suddenly, Stevenson turned the power off, and the screen went black. "Let's eat something. We can talk more after. I want to hear what you're going to talk about in Chicago."

He rose from his chair and walked to a cupboard. "You'll have to forgive me. All I have is Dry food and water." He produced a jug of water, cups, bowls, and a plastic bag full of green chips.

"Stevenson, why do you eat Dry food?" Anderson asked.

"Yeah, I know, I can get wholesome food from the Underground. But when I eat Dry food, my face turns blue, and the Chinese don't suspect me of being an Underground leader."

I looked closely at Stevenson's face. Indeed, it did have a tint of blue. I hadn't noticed it before.

"Your fear is legitimate," Anderson said. "They know the leaders are the heart of the organization. If they ever decide to crack down, it'll be the leaders they seek out first. Our faces can give us away."

"I haven't eaten real food in ten years," Stevenson said. "All I eat now is Dry food, twice a day. As I understand it, my life expectancy is fifty-five. If I'm lucky, I'll make it to sixty. So be it."

He filled his small bowl full of chips and passed the bag to me. I did the same and passed it to Anderson, who smiled at me and nodded it was okay. We munched on the green chips. They actually tasted good. I suppose if you're going to force people to eat the same thing every day, it had better taste good.

We talked for a few hours, discussing what we knew about God, the meaning of life, and the current state of enlightenment. Stevenson reiterated that society had become highly spiritual. The concept of reincarnation was widely accepted, and people understood that they were eternal beings. As a group, society was close to being enlightened. This was not readily apparent, because in places like America, where spirituality was suppressed, it appeared as if spiritual enlightenment was years away from reaching fruition.

* * * * *

In the morning, Stevenson drove us to the city's airport on the isolated outskirts of town. As we arrived, I was surprised by his nonchalance. He didn't say a word as he drove up to the security gate, calmly looked at the camera and punched in a secret code. The gate swung open, and we drove through.

"This is where I work," he said, in a calm, reassuring voice. "I've arranged a flight for you in a cargo plane. The security here is very lax. There's never been a detected breach of security. Like I said yesterday, we are passive. The Chinese take it for granted that we will behave."

We drove onto the expanse of asphalt and concrete. It wasn't a 20th-century airport. Missing were commuters and a terminal. I didn't see a single person. Also missing

Chapter Four - Chicago

were any small airplanes. Those on the tarmac were long and sleek, somewhat like a Concorde.

Stevenson parked outside a hangar, and we went inside. Two men in yellow silk jumpsuits met us. They smiled and greeted us warmly. They had been expecting us.

"The plane is loaded and ready to go," one of them said.

Stevenson nodded, then looked at Anderson and me. "Erickson will help you find a jumpsuit and put you on the plane. When you get to Chicago, someone will be waiting for you."

"Thank you for everything," Anderson said.

Stevenson smiled and shook our hands. "I hope your journey goes well. Good luck."

Erickson led us to an enclosed locker for our jumpsuits. From the bright colors available, we both selected orange and put the lightweight jumpsuits on over our clothes.

"These are government-issued," Erickson said. "You'll look like government workers." He paused, then looked at me. "You're the one from the 20th century! We've been waiting for you for two hundred years. It's a pleasure to meet you. I hope your journey goes well."

I looked at Anderson. "Is this what I can expect?"

He nodded.

I looked back at Erickson. "What exactly have you been waiting for?"

"A prophecy in the 21st century said that a man from the past would come when it was time. He would be an ordinary man, who would carry a message of truth that would free the people. He wouldn't appear for many years, as we struggled to find spiritual truth. Near the end of our struggle, he would appear and show us the light. From what I've heard, you seem to be that man."

I smiled. "I'm not sure about any prophecy. I suppose I fit the criteria. I am a stranger from the past, and I do carry a spiritual message."

"You're him. I can feel it," Erickson said, smiling.

I smiled back. "Maybe. I always think of prophecy as a possibility. There is always some truth in prophecy, though generally, it's not what we expect. For instance, I could be one of several strangers from the past who has come to spread knowledge. The prophecy doesn't necessarily mean only one man. Or it could refer to someone so different that people perceive him to be from the past. We have to have an open mind when considering prophecy. Erickson, I hope the prophecy is fulfilled, and I hope it is soon, during your lifetime."

Erickson smiled. "Me too. Okay, let's go." He pointed for us to get into the small transport vehicle used for loading planes. As he drove us to the plane, he was silent in contemplation. I sensed his strong desire for freedom and that there were many more like him in Chicago.

The supersonic plane got us there in less than an hour. Airplane technology was one of the technologies that had advanced since the 20th century. Many technologies, Anderson said, had actually regressed. The Chinese and other world leaders were more concerned with maintaining power and the status quo than finding new technologies to advance civilization.

Once on the ground, we waited for what we hoped would be friendly faces. Much to our dismay, no one arrived. We sat for nearly an hour, strapped to our seats, perilously waiting. Finally, we heard voices outside and

Chapter Four - Chicago

the bay door opened. In stepped the receiving party, whom Anderson instantly recognized.

"Henderson, what took you so long? We've been waiting an hour."

Henderson laughed. "One hour, Andy? I've been waiting a lifetime to meet this man, and you can't wait an hour?"

The two others with Henderson joined in his laughter. Both were dressed in conservative suits and looked like professors.

I looked at Anderson. "You better tell these guys that I'm just a normal guy from the 20th century. I'm no messiah."

They looked at me, then at Anderson.

"Meet John," Anderson said. We all shook hands and exchanged greetings. "He's not a messiah any more than we are. Please stop all this talk of a prophecy. It's making him uncomfortable."

Henderson nodded. "Sure. Now let's get off this airplane and away from the airport. A van is waiting for us. We're going to my living quarters. You'll be staying with me."

We walked down the cargo ramp to a futuristic van with windows everywhere and seating for ten people, with plenty of room for the five of us. Several airplanes in the distance were similar to the one we had arrived in. I didn't see any small airplanes here, either.

After we left the airport, the lack of people caught my attention. The number of people on the streets was minimal, like back in Fayetteville.

We headed up South Michigan Avenue. The street was vaguely familiar. If someone had asked me how to get to the Sears Tower, I could have given them directions.

As in Fayetteville, everything here had aged. The buildings looked positively ancient. Although the streets were clean, there wasn't a single new structure.

"Where are all the people?" I asked.

"The Chinese don't allow loitering," Henderson replied.

"Or shopping," Anderson added.

"That's right," Henderson continued talking as he drove. "All shopping is done by computer. Only those who have business may be on the streets. We're driving in a government vehicle, so we're considered 'on business.' There are cameras and microphones throughout the city. If the Chinese suspect anyone of breaking the law, they do spot checks. For instance, this monitor on the dashboard could turn on at any moment, with a Chinese face asking for our IDs."

"How do they do it?" I asked.

"Infrared. We have invisible tattoos on top of our right hands. There's a scanner inside the monitor. We would be asked to hold up our right hand in front of the monitor."

"Are we at risk right now?" I asked. "As you know, I don't have a tattoo."

"No," he replied. "It's rare to spot-check government employees. I've never been ID-checked in a government vehicle."

Anderson added. "Until you give your first speech, there's little to worry about. Only a select few even know you're here, John, and they won't inform the Chinese."

"How are the IDs used?" I asked Henderson.

"You name it. Checking in at work, buying over the computer, paying a doctor, taking the subway, for just about everything."

Chapter Four - Chicago

"Then they monitor all of the population closely here in Chicago?" I asked.

The two men behind Anderson and me laughed. Henderson simply nodded, then added, "They keep a file on everyone, and they are constantly adding information to it. The Chinese know about our lives. They use our IDs to create a historical record. They know almost everything we do."

He turned into the underground garage of what appeared to be a hotel. Not many vehicles were inside. Those I saw had similar government markings.

"This is where I live," Henderson said. "Most of the tenants are government employees. As a group, all government employees are considered a low security risk. We are conformists. We follow the rules."

Henderson found a place to park.

"What's the tradeoff?" I asked. "Does this mean that government workers are given special privileges?"

Henderson smiled. "Indeed. We're given adequate living quarters and access to amenities that the public is denied. For instance, we get foreign television and, on occasion, access to real food. You might say that we're part of the elite of society, or what you called the middle class in the late 20th century. It's so advantageous to work for the government that people acquiesce to becoming part of the authoritarian rule."

We stepped out of the van and went to the elevator to take us up to Henderson's living quarters. As the elevator hummed upward, I asked, "Why did you work for the government?"

He paused and looked at the two men with him. One of them answered. "We of the Underground join in order to have a cover. You might say that we're spies."

The elevator stopped, and we exited. Like much of the infrastructure, the hallway was ancient. A distinct trail in the dirty red carpet led the way down the corridor. The grimy, whitewashed walls were scuffed and chipped, and an unpleasant smell of decay pervaded the building.

His apartment was the size of a small hotel room. This was adequate? It wasn't squalid, like Stevenson's house in Fayetteville, but it was old, very old.

"Have a seat," Henderson said. "We have some questions for you."

I looked at Anderson. His face showed no expression, and he remained silent.

"These two gentlemen are historians," Henderson said, pointing to the other two men who had come with us from the airport. "The Underground leadership wants them to question you about your lifetime. Records from the hospital where you were picked up were destroyed, so we can't confirm your story. I'm sorry we have to do this."

One of the historians said, "This should be easy and painless. We're just going to ask a few simple questions that anyone would know who lived in the 1980s."

I looked at Anderson.

He said, "It's okay, John. The questions are simple. I tried to convince them, but they wouldn't listen to me. I'm only one. The others wanted to do this test."

I nodded.

They asked me 20 questions. I quickly answered all of them easily. Which were the most populated states? Who was elected President in 1980? What is politically correct speech?

I asked them if I passed. They nodded, and the tension in the room evaporated.

Chapter Four - Chicago

"Being historians," one of the men added, "we would also like to talk about your lifetime. This isn't part of the test. We just want to have a conversation. Is that okay?"

"Sure. What do you want to know?"

"What caused the U.S. economy to falter and stop growing? America was the dominant economy and world power. Then suddenly, it stopped growing. In your opinion, what happened?"

I smiled. "You guys go right for the important information. I like that." The two historians regarded me blankly. They did not smile back, nor did they show any body language that implied informality.

"Well, you know most of this. We've read the same history. However, I will give you my opinion.

"The U.S. made bad choices on economic policy, relying on debt for economic growth and ignoring the onset of a perpetual decline in oil production, which was commonly referred to as peak oil," I said.

"It all started with Republican President Ronald Reagan's voodoo economics and his global free trade focus in the 1980s. When he came into office, the U.S. government debt was less than one trillion. He cut taxes and began deficit spending on a massive scale. His policies led to vibrant economic growth, which continued through the 1990s and into the first decade of the 21st century."

Henderson got up out of his seat and went to look out the window. He was not interested in my answers. The two historians continued to take notes and maintain their same posture of seriousness. They were like FBI agents.

"The budget and trade deficits ballooned in the 1980s and then exploded in the early 21st century. Nobody thought this was an issue, and we continued to accumulate debt. They were wrong. By 2025, the debt had reached thirty-five trillion. It was simply a matter of time before the dollar collapsed and the economy hit a wall. With so many dollars held by foreigners, we were at their mercy to hold our debt, and purchase more.

"When enough foreigners decided to stop purchasing our treasury bonds and to also sell our debt, we had no recourse but to default on our debt, and basically declare bankruptcy. It was inevitable, although few expected it, right up until the day it happened.

"It's simple to understand. The U.S. economy was based on debt and easy credit. From 1980 until 2025, we borrowed trillions of dollars from foreigners to maintain our standard of living. However, once the bill collector showed up, we didn't have any money to pay them back. We tried to use the lunacy of MMT, modern monetary theory, that implied that debt didn't matter since we could print any amount of money we needed. It's amazing that this theory came into existence. Actually, it was created by politicians and not economists. It allowed government to pump the economy with digitally printed money whenever the economy slowed, but that was a doomed policy.

"It is really easy to understand. As a country, we lived beyond our means for an extended period of time until it faltered. Once the economy faltered from the stranglehold of debt, the lower and middle classes were left in dire straits. Many felt betrayed by capitalism and politicians who had promised prosperity and opportunity. This led people to lose faith in America, and America's future. Money and materialism had been the heartbeat of America. Now there was nothing left for the people to believe in. Thus, the economic breakdown became even more profound on a social and cultural level."

Chapter Four - Chicago

I took a sip of water and then continued. "Not only did people give up on capitalism and consumerism, but they also gave up on being the shining light to the world. We gave up and retrenched. We stopped supporting the world with armed troops and financial assistance. We brought our troops home and became isolationists.

"Once the economy imploded, we didn't even have a strong manufacturing base to fall back on. From the year 2000 until 2005, China built seventy thousand manufacturing plants. During this time, three million manufacturing jobs were lost in the United States. And this trend continued. It was a stupid policy to give away all of those jobs to China and Asia.

"Unions were our undoing. That is what led to the breakup of the country by weakening the economy to a shell of its former self. Unions prevented companies from competing as a team. Instead, unions created conflict between management and workers. Instead of allowing manufacturing to flourish, we chose to let it die by allowing unions to exist.

"My grandfather once told me that unions would ruin this nation, and he was right. Instead of allowing unions, corporations should have flattened the pay scale and paid workers a fair wage, and also given them profit sharing. Corporate America was too consumed with historical precedence, where the C-suite gets the best salaries and bonuses.

"In addition to outlawing unions, we should have required foreign companies to make a portion of their products here. It mystified me that we gave foreign corporations a free pass to our market, which was the largest in the world. Why not require large corporations like Samsung and Panasonic to at least have one manufacturing plant in the U.S.?"

I paused.

"How did high oil prices affect the economy?" a historian asked.

"The world reached its maximum oil production, including natural gas liquids, in 2025 at around one hundred million barrels per day. Since oil and cheap energy are the lifeblood of the economy, it was destined to have an impact. The fact that the U.S. was already broke from too much debt, made high energy prices impossible to overcome. It was the perfect storm."

I paused and looked at Henderson. "Do you have any water?"

"Sure," he said. He went into the kitchen and returned with the cold glass of water, which he placed next to me.

I took a large drink and then continued. "Before the U.S. economy hit its wall, it began creating bubbles from the enormous amount of money printing. That money had to go somewhere. The first bubble was the dot-com bubble in the 1990s, which burst in 1999. The second bubble was the housing bubble in the early 2000s, which burst in 2008, and was known as the Great Financial Crisis. The final bubble, which was called the Everything Bubble, burst in 2024. That was the year we hit the wall."

"What a mess, and most of it was avoidable," a historian remarked.

I nodded.

"Why didn't we make better choices?" a historian asked.

"People were caught up in the illusion that America was invincible, and politicians fell in love with MMT. Also, making dramatic changes was never something that was

Chapter Four - Chicago

really possible. For instance, the U.S. was the only western country that didn't have universal health care. We needed it, but our political system was not set up for big changes like that.

"Also, Reaganomics convinced us that prosperity was directly linked to economic growth and globalism, and everyone bought into that. Growth and globalism was our friend, and that was the Holy Grail we followed. Let's not forget, that even when things were looking dire after the GFC, no one wanted to change directions on our free trade policies. Nearly all of our politicians, right up until we hit the wall, wanted to follow the same free trade, globalist, pro-growth policies."

"Did spirituality play a role in all this economic turmoil?" a historian asked. "After all, the country ended up becoming much more spiritual after the economic troubles."

"I would say no. Americans were still very secular and materialistic during this timeframe. In fact, corporations and Wall Street had a preeminent influence. Gnostic ideas of sustainability didn't have a voice in setting our economic policies until after the collapse."

I paused to let my audience absorb some of the history before tackling the next subject.

"We can't ignore the fact that there was a chasm between spirituality and technology in the 20th century," I said.

"The technological advancements from 1900 through the end of the 20th century to 2000 were incredible to behold. The changes were staggering. By the end of the 20th century, society had advanced technologically to the point where we relied on machines. Compare that to 1900, when society was technologically barren. Air conditioning, radio, and television were still decades away from being invented.

"By the time I was cryogenically suspended in 1994, the computer and electronics had transformed the world. The advent of the computer in the 1950s was revolutionary. The computer allowed us to put satellites beyond the planet's atmosphere. By the 1960s, satellites ringed the planet in geostationary orbit. The world rapidly became connected electronically. Computers changed the world. We could not have gone to the moon in the 1960s, nor had airplanes that allowed international travel to nearly any city, without them, not to mention the advent of the Internet in the 1990s."

I paused in contemplation. "We know that the world advanced technologically at an incredible rate in the 20th century. How did this lead to the degeneration of society? Where freedoms were lost, education declined, and homelessness became pervasive? Perhaps it had something to do with the fact that the advance in spirituality didn't keep pace. We went from no air travel to space travel in less than one hundred years. During this dramatic advance in technology, our spiritual advancement nearly stood still. There were a few spiritual changes in society, such as feminism, civil rights, social legislation, and ecology. On the whole, however, spiritual beliefs were basically the same throughout the 20th century. For instance, the growth in Gnostic spirituality was only a tiny portion of the population. Most Americans, especially those in power, still believed the Bible was the final word.

"The chasm between technology and spirituality grew larger and larger as the 20th century progressed. In the second half of the century, the lack of spirituality began to manifest. Technology changed our lives and exposed

Chapter Four – Chicago

the lack of a spiritual foundation in society. For instance, mass communication made it possible for everyone to see the disparities that existed between the affluent and less fortunate. People weren't treated equally, and it was impossible to deny this fact. The American Dream was exposed as more of a myth than reality. If you were born poor, then you usually remained poor."

I paused. "Is this getting boring? We can talk about something else if you want."

"Please continue," one of the historians said. "We are interested in this question."

They sat listening and watching me without emotion. They didn't care for small talk and were interested only in gathering information. I felt like I was a book they were reading. The conversation was one-sided and impersonal. They didn't care about me, only what I knew.

"Okay," I continued, "as technology advanced, so did the economy. By the 1950s, the American standard of living was the envy of the world. Technology created economic prosperity never before achieved. The result of economic prosperity was a new middle class, which was a major social change for society. This group of people became the mainstream, the agenda-setters who determined the status quo. The 1950s, along with the emergence of the middle class, marked the beginning of societal materialism. As a nation, we decided that economic growth was good, and that materialism and prosperity went hand-in-hand. Thus, was born the age of the consumer. The idea of equity and equality were always an afterthought. Some people achieved, and some didn't.

"Prosperity and affluence became the American dream to which all aspired. Thus, economic growth became the single most important value in society. The economy steadily grew as we focused on growth. By the year 2000, the gross national product had reached eight trillion dollars. From 1950 to 2000, America's economy grew nearly five percent every year."

One of the historians asked, "During this focus on economic growth, what happened to spirituality?"

I smiled. "That's what I am trying to explain, but I wanted to explain the subtext first. Economics, not spirituality, was the foundation of society. For this reason, spirituality remained stuck in old dogma and couldn't evolve. Society was mired in old beliefs. People didn't believe they were God, quite the opposite. For this reason, society placed value on the wrong thing.

"We valued prosperity, and this focus created a negative outcome: debt, which led to economic stagnation. Moreover, society grew in negative ways from our economic focus: crime, drugs, child abuse, spousal abuse, greed, violence, gangs, pornography, and prejudice. The list is long. This negativity wasn't the result of sin or the devil. It was from our beliefs. We believed in the wrong things, mainly the God of economic prosperity."

I waited for one of the historians to respond.

"So, a focus on economic growth led to beliefs that created degeneration? Instead of evolving spiritually, society evolved economically until that was no longer possible."

I nodded. "Yes. Materialism and the American dream became the same thing. Thus, we became preoccupied with individual and family achievement and lost sight of the impact on humanity from that focus. We had created a dog-eat-dog world with a myriad of winners and losers.

"People wanted nice things and a high standard of living. It didn't matter if everyone couldn't have them.

Chapter Four - Chicago

People believed that growth created the opportunity for everyone. This was a big lie.

"A family, a big house, a nice car, a large bank account, plus respect for achievements. This is what everyone desired. Those who achieved it felt they deserved it, and that it was a blessing from God. Those who didn't achieve it were actually judged as lacking, and many were even labeled as losers. For this reason, panhandling was outlawed in many cities. The homeless were treated as pariahs, with taunts like, 'Get a job!'

"People became identified with their achievement. Who you were was directly correlated with your success. More than that, everyone was judged by achievements. Whatever we did to earn income was our achievement. And if it wasn't worthy, then we weren't worthy. In fact, it was implied that it was our fault if we weren't achieving.

"The better our achievement, the more status society granted us. We valued economic growth, and achievement made us feel proud. That's why wealthy people, entertainers, athletes, and others in the public eye became celebrities. They were the elite achievers. They had achieved their dreams. They were deemed worthy and granted eminence ..."

One of the historians interrupted. "What was the fallout from this focus on achievement?"

"It led to a focus on separation and individuality, which was the exact opposite of spirituality. Humanity can't flourish without recognizing that we are all God. The focus on separation leads to judgment, manipulation, prejudice, and selfishness. All of these deceitful values flourished during the American era. It became apparent during this time of economic stagnation that the foundation of our values and spirituality was lacking, and a change was needed.

"From materialism, selfishness became the norm. For instance, at the end of 1993, the most important political issue was crime. Everyone wanted to be protected from the underachievers. The crime bill in 1994 gave federal money to individual states for more police officers. The achievers wanted to be protected. This was the epitome of a society that lacked spirituality. The crime bill revealed our true social priorities. Instead of focusing on the homeless problem, or the inequality of the school system, we got a crime bill."

I reached over and took another drink from my glass of water.

"Society didn't recognize crime as a symptom of a bigger problem. Instead, people clamored for more policemen and stronger penalties for crimes. The majority of Americans surveyed agreed with the 'three strikes,' get-tough legislation for repeat offenders. The 'three strikes' legislation passed in many states. People who didn't achieve lost their human rights. Three repeat offenses, and they went to prison for life. Thus, human rights were defined by an achievement scale.

"It should be noted that about fifteen years after the 1994 crime bill was passed, the inner cities began defunding the police. They had finally had enough of the focus on materialism, since they were not the beneficiaries."

"What about technology?" One of the historians asked. "How did it impact the denigration of society?"

I smiled. "Technology became the great equalizer. Technology forced us to become more spiritual. The more we denied our spirituality, the more technology exposed

Chapter Four – Chicago

our lack of spirituality. Steadily, our societal values became exposed.

"Mass communication made this possible. When executives were getting paid four hundred times the average salary, everyone knew. When women were being discriminated against in corporations and law firms, everyone knew. When one-third of black men had been in jail or on probation, everyone knew. With the advent of mass communication, nothing could be hidden. Information flowed freely. Technology steadily made this flow of information that much easier.

"Technology jobs required education, and the better-educated people in society had an advantage getting a job in these professions. Minorities and the lower classes were at a disadvantage because their schools were lacking. This created a chasm that exposed the illusion of equality and fairness in society. The chasm was exposed by the mass media, but most people, including our politicians, did nothing.

"Technology exposed our spiritual values as lacking. We were building a suburban, materialistic society that was not sustainable. It was becoming obvious to many that a shift in spirituality was needed to bring humanity closer together and create more harmony."

I smiled. "That was fun, but that's all I have time for tonight. I need to prepare for tomorrow's speech."

Anderson looked at the historians. "John's speech tomorrow night will be recorded in both audio and video. Our hope is that people will learn from him and become catalysts for our freedom."

Everyone looked at me.

I shrugged. "I guess that's why I'm here."

CHAPTER FIVE

The Speech

The next night, I stood in the lobby of an old, musty movie theater with Anderson, Henderson, and several of their friends. It smelled of dirt and decay, and the windows had been boarded up years ago.

The venue was small by design because anything larger could attract the attention of the Chinese. Anderson was concerned about a public gathering, but Henderson said the Underground had used this building several times without raising suspicion.

We met people as they entered. Anticipation and excitement filled the air. They arrived slowly, passing through the lobby to find a seat. Everyone had been specifically invited. Many had traveled from outlying areas, under dangerous circumstances, some even from distant states.

One man had traveled from Denver. He was very small, and only weighed about 75 pounds, and stood less than five feet tall. His incredibly intelligent eyes mesmerized me. Anderson said he was another leader from the Underground and we would see him in Denver, which was our next destination.

Finally, it was time. Everyone was in his seat.

Anderson walked to the podium and waited for the noise to subside.

"Good evening, ladies and gentlemen. Tonight is truly an incredible night. Many of us have hoped for this during our lifetime, to see a sign that peace and freedom are near. I believe that tonight we have that sign."

Everyone applauded.

"You know why we are gathered. The man who will speak tonight is not one of us. He is from another time. He was alive during the late 20th century, the period immediately before the Chinese invasion. I have lived with him now for more than two weeks, and I can say that he is authentic, and he has come to help."

There was more applause.

Anderson continued. "We know from history that the Age of Aquarius started in the early 21st century. John Randall is one of those who began the transition into the Age of Aquarius. He contributed to the spiritual philosophy that we follow today. In fact, I have a book in my library that he wrote in the 20th century.

"We don't know how much influence John had on our spiritual philosophy, but I think he's going to have a huge impact on our freedom. I believe God delivered John to us for this purpose. I present to you, John Randall."

Everyone stood and applauded.

Feeling honored and welcomed, I approached the podium and smiled. I had to wait nearly 20 seconds for the applause to subside.

"It feels good to be here tonight. Before I begin, I want to thank the people who arranged this event and who organized this trip. Many have gone to extremes for our benefit, and I want to thank them. I also want to thank all of you for coming."

I scanned the audience. In the front row, a man sitting next to Anderson and Henderson was filming me with

Chapter Five - The Speech

a small video camera attached to a tripod. I wondered if those in the back could hear me because I wasn't using a microphone.

"Can everyone hear me in the back?" I asked.

"Yes," a voice boomed. "We can hear you fine."

I nodded, took a deep breath, and began.

"I should probably begin with a short introduction of who I am. I'm not from this timeline. The period I lived in was the height of the American era. We were the envy of the world, with the highest standard of living. In fact, one-quarter of the economic output of the entire planet came from the United States. We also consumed one-quarter of all of the world's energy supplies. You would have thought I would have been proud to be an American during that era. Far from it. The problem was spirituality. It was lacking to a high degree.

"The problem was that America did not believe that they were God. I *knew* that I was God, or at least that God was part of my soul, and that we were connected. America was built on the belief that we were separate from God. This was obvious to me and the other New Agers. We tried our best to expose others to this truth, but it was not easy. There was an ingrained belief in Christianity and the concept of separation, and that was not going away easily.

"Today, you face your own problems. Many of you feel the same frustrations that I felt. I say to you to persevere and continue the good fight. I spent my life getting as close to God as I possibly could and to convey my spiritual awareness through my example and through my writing. I believe that has led me to you today. God sent me into the future to a time when I could be of use. I say to you to persevere: to get closer to God and share your spiritual awareness by your example, and to bring God down to this plane of existence.

"How do you do that? Well, you become a frequency of love. This is done in two steps. The first step is to find your soul – your higher self – and have a close relationship with it. You do this by quietening your mind and listening to your heart. You have to learn how to communicate with your higher self and allow it to guide you.

"A good starting point for quietening your mind is meditating. Ideally, you want to always be meditating, with your ego constantly quiet. Once you begin your relationship with your higher self, you will know what I am talking about.

"Once that relationship is in place, you can move to step two. This is when you live life from a place of neutrality, a place of unconditional love. You accept everything that happens in your life with constant gratitude. You recognize that life only gives you two things: blessings and opportunities. If you think you are getting something else, then it is an illusion.

"If you use these two steps, then you will become a frequency of love and spread light to those around you. If enough people spread their light, love will manifest on the planet. That's how you create peace on Earth."

I paused, and people applauded.

"Thank you. I have found that the most important thing to understand is that *we* are God, and that there is no separation between God and us. God created us, but not as separate entities apart from God. Nothing, absolutely nothing, is separate from God. God is *All That Is*. We are God. *We* are eternal. And since we are eternal, our lives are perfect."

I paused.

Chapter Five - The Speech

"Everyone in this room is an eternal soul, and this life, and all of our past and future lives, are *perfect*. God has no blemish. Thus, *we* have no blemish. It is only illusion and a lack of awareness that keeps us from realizing this.

"The Bible states that the Golden Rule is to love our neighbors as if they are ourselves. That rule is actually wrong, but humanity wasn't ready for the truth, so God had to improvise. The actual Golden Rule is to love your neighbor because they are yourself. I bring you God's other Golden Rule: Never force your will upon another. Thus, allow all humans their sovereignty.

"Essentially, these mean the same thing, and that we must love each other unconditionally. We must not only love those we know, but also strangers and everyone with whom we come into contact.

"How important are these rules? So important that it literally creates our experience. How? That's the topic of my talk tonight.

"God is all pervasive, and God reacts to our beliefs, thoughts, intent, and actions. God is aware of all our beliefs, thoughts, intent, and actions. Even the most insignificant of these creates reverberations. Not only in this life, but the next. We don't need to manipulate someone to infringe upon their will. All we have to do is think it.

"Thought is energy. Thought and intent are the power behind everything. Our thoughts literally create our lives and affect others. When we think thoughts that infringe upon the will of others, we go against one of God's universal laws, thereby creating karma for ourselves. Everything is recorded in the Akashic records, which is God's record book. Everything that ever happens is recorded. Thus, our lives are spent accumulating karma.

And since we are eternal, there's plenty of time to clear our karma."

I moved to the left and closer to the audience. "For example, if you are mean to your children, those experiences are tallied into the Akashic records and are added to your soul's karma. That karma has to be addressed in some manner for the soul to grow. That is the whole purpose of incarnating. Life is one long journey of accumulating and addressing karma until you reach enlightenment, which is one with God. Life is a journey home, but it takes a long time."

I moved back to the center of the stage. "God is always listening. We and our thoughts are a part of God. When we understand that completely, we become enlightened. Once we are aware of these two rules, we stop creating karma and begin to clear the karma from our past."

I moved away from the podium to remove the barrier between the audience and me. I smiled and opened my arms. "*We* are aspects of God. This is hard to conceptualize because we don't feel omnipotent. But what about our thoughts? Thoughts can be omnipotent. Thoughts are energy. Thoughts are as real as we are. Our thoughts are aspects of us, much like we are aspects of God. In essence, our thoughts are God's ideas, and our ideas create reality.

"Our ideas create because God is always listening. God perceives every thought by every consciousness. This is inevitable because God *is* that consciousness. Again, our feelings of being separate from God and separate from each other are an illusion. God is *All* and interacts with All. God uses our ideas to rearrange our experiences. That's what life is all about: God's ideas.

"Essentially, everyone is a co-creator with God. Our beliefs create emotions and thoughts, which lead to

Chapter Five - The Speech

experience. Nothing, absolutely nothing, can happen to us unless it's a product of our beliefs. Everyone literally creates their own reality by their beliefs. Nothing happens to anyone by accident. We cannot stub our toe unless that is in our belief system."

I moved to the right and looked at those in the first row. "This is why destiny is real. We come into this life with an agenda and lessons to learn. Our agenda fits the family and environment we chose. We then use this agenda and our beliefs to create our life. God places us into a situation where our agenda is possible to achieve. All we have to do is use our intent and follow our passion. It is all perfect. It is all there for the taking. The tricky part is finding the right path to achieve our agenda."

"What people fail to realize is that we are co-creators with God. Everyone is like a giant magnet, attracting experience by their beliefs and intent. This not only happens to individuals, but to societies as well. A society's experience is the result of its members' *combined* beliefs. In essence, we create our reality in conjunction with God."

I looked at a woman in the first row. "Am I making sense?"

She nodded.

"Should I continue?"

A chorus of 'yes' moved through the theater.

I smiled. "That's the last time I'll ask."

Many laughed.

I stared at the audience in contemplation. "What are we talking about? God. And what is God? *All That Is*. And what are God's two rules? Love your neighbor and treat them fairly. You can combine these into one rule, which is to live by unconditional love. When we do not impinge our will upon another, we are loving that person unconditionally. And guess what? God likes that. Why? Because God is love and harmony. Love and harmony are the core of God and are our natural tendency. In fact, it is our destiny. Love and harmony are inevitable for everyone, albeit not necessarily in this lifetime.

"What I am going to say next is the most important thing I will say tonight. Everything on this plane of reality and on the etheric spiritual planes is based on love and harmony. On the etheric planes, love and harmony are a natural occurrence. On the physical plane, it is either in existence or it is evolving toward its existence.

"Do you understand? God only knows love and harmony. And if love and harmony do not exist, then God will make it exist. However long it takes.

"So, since God knows the outcome, everything that leads to that outcome is perfect. When we deny a situation, a person, or ourselves as a perfect idea, we are denying God's perfection. In fact, we are denying God's existence. How many of you do this every day?" A few raised their hands.

"What am I saying? God only knows perfection. This means that everything in this world is perfect. Universal law implies that we cannot judge God's ideas, the good ones or the bad ones. God's law implies that we must love unconditionally or else be unenlightened.

"The Bible says that man is fallen and lives in sin. At the time it was written, that was all that humankind could grasp. It is false. It is a lie. Most of the big ideas from the Bible are false. The idea that we are God wasn't something humanity was ready for two thousand years ago."

I scanned the audience. Everyone was sitting attentively in their seats. "I see some in the audience who aren't comfortable with the concept of perfection. What

Chapter Five - The Speech

ideas are not acceptable to you? Perhaps, the Chinese ruling this country? As far as God is concerned, all ideas are perfect. If we decide that any idea is not perfect, we are breaking God's law. We are invalidating the Chinese as separate from us, which is not true.

"Then what can be done? The answer is to stop believing that the Chinese are separate from you. The answer is to seek something that is in harmony with God's love. We tell the Chinese that we honor and love them. However, we also tell them that we have decided to live in more harmony with less oppression. And that we seek something that is in accord with our spiritual beliefs of oneness. After enough people align their beliefs with this intent, it will happen. God will honor our beliefs. If that is what we truly want, God will make it happen. That's how it works.

"God manifests peace and harmony to the degree that we love unconditionally. It's that simple. The more we love unconditionally, the more peace and harmony we will have in our lives. Conversely, the less we love unconditionally, the more negative manifestations we have.

"When we manifest peace and harmony in our lives, it spreads from there. That's all we can do. We only have control over ourselves. Let everyone else do what they want. Allow people their free will. Understand that everyone is a perfect idea. Our job is to also be a perfect idea. We can live by setting an example, and not by telling others how to live, including the Chinese." A few nodded, but not everyone was convinced.

"God's law is simple," I restated. "Do not infringe on *any* of God's ideas. If you don't like the idea, then create a new one. When we look at another human being, we are seeing God; we are seeing another of God's ideas. We all must coexist with the awareness that we are all interrelated, and that we are all one. That's how we love. If everywhere we look, we see God, then love is the natural outcome. And when we follow this law, it happens automatically.

"Peace and harmony exist when we are aware that everything is God, and everything is a perfect idea of God. It's easy to perceive ideas as less than perfect. We've been conditioned to believe that peace and harmony are good, but that everything else is not good. This duality actually prevents peace and harmony. Why? Because the minute we judge an idea as less than perfect, we are denying God, and perceiving less-than-perfect ideas as separate from God.

"This may sound bizarre. You may even be saying to yourself, 'No way. How can the Chinese domination be a perfect idea?' Believe me, it's all an illusion. You are creating this domination for some lessons that you all need to learn. Once you are done with your lessons, you will create something new.

"Every soul on this planet we come into contact with has lived hundreds or thousands of lives on the physical plane. This planet is nothing more than a school for advanced souls. Any other perception is simply an illusion. The Chinese are God in disguise. We just don't see it.

"During my era, there was a guy named Gandhi who, through sheer spiritual strength and non-violence, freed his country. It was an amazing display of spirituality. He treated his repressors as his equal and as misguided. When they put him in prison, he cleaned the restrooms with a smile on his face. He never lost sight of his true spirit.

"You have to be like Gandhi. You have to treat your oppressors as your equals. In fact, they are more than that.

Chapter Five - The Speech

They are your brothers. All humans are one spirit. That is something we must all hold close to our hearts.

"Many, or most of you, believe the Chinese are denying your freedom. Well, the Chinese can't take away your freedom. Only you can take away your freedom by believing it is so. You are currently on a trip away from home. The purpose of the trip is to learn something new. It has nothing to do with freedom or happiness. The journey is about your soul.

"The only reason we can't accept the Chinese as a perfect idea is our belief in duality, because we've been conditioned to believe in right and wrong. We think we're right, and they're wrong. Our beliefs create conflict, instead of harmony. They create a stalemate.

"God is complex. As such, life is complex. But we needn't worry about the complexity. All we need to do is follow God's rules. In the end, we will all learn about the complexity of God. That's what reincarnation is all about. God's idea of a soul, and the reason we were created, is to learn about God. And that's what we do: we experience, we learn, and we become spiritually aware.

"Before each life, we choose what we need to learn, and we carefully pre-plan our lives. Things don't always go according to our plan. But even if they don't, the result is still perfect. We get out of each life as much as we can, and that's enough. Since we are eternal, it doesn't matter how fast we learn. We have plenty of time to learn our lessons.

"It's not so much that we pre-plan our lives, but that we choose them. You see, everything has already happened. We are just playing rewind. When we are in between lives, we select our next life based on what we need to learn. This actually gets really complicated. First, when you select a life, everyone that you are going to live with has to agree. For this lifetime, I had to ask twenty-seven families before I found a match. The reason it was so difficult is that the people I generally incarnate with did not want to experience the late 20th century. For an advanced old soul, it was not a pleasant experience. In fact, it felt like a prison, much like what you experience today.

"Once you do select a life, it has multiple variations. The themes will be similar, but you have choices to select from. In other words, your wife is not predetermined. There are some women who are more predisposed, but you will have choices. The same goes for your profession and your spirituality. However, you can't change your inherent nature, and thus, the lessons you come to learn will play out no matter what choices you make. In other words, you pretty much know in advance what you are coming to learn.

"The reason we doubt that our lives are perfect is because we doubt our divinity. We forget who we are, which is God. Another reason for this doubt stems from our belief in duality. We deny that imperfection is an illusion. We refuse to believe in perfection. We think that our lives should be better, instead of accepting them as already perfect.

"One of the things that was difficult for me to understand was that everything is divinely ordered. In fact, it was recommended for me to do two things to help with my spiritual progress. One, find something to do that I am passionate about, and that gives me satisfaction and joy. Two, accept that the world is divinely ordered and that you don't need to control the outcome. Number two was much more difficult to do than number one. Letting go and trusting the universe is very hard."

Chapter Five - The Speech

I smiled, and several people laughed.

"I haven't discussed morality because it is a big subject, and we only have so much time tonight. But I will say this. To God, evil is just another aspect of life. And since God is love, love will always overwhelm evil. Evil is temporary. Evil arises, and then it diminishes. Evil's eventual demise is inevitable, and those who experience it, learn from it. Evil arises when we go against God's laws. It's the outcome of ego and free will, and God allows it so that we can learn. The key takeaway is that evil is an idea, and all ideas are perfect. If someone chooses to learn through evil, that is their choice. God allows it."

I paused. "Many of you are thinking, how can he say that every idea is perfect, while at the same time stating that God has laws?"

I smiled. Many smiled back.

"God's laws bring us back home, but they don't prevent us from running away from home. Remember earlier when I told you the most important thing? Which was that love and harmony are the basis for life and that everything is trending toward love and harmony. Well, we can experience evil because it is temporary and not the final part of the journey.

"Life is complicated and has many apparent contradictions. If it weren't complicated, life wouldn't be so interesting. God isn't boring. Neither is life. The complexity of life makes it fun to figure out. That's why it requires so many lifetimes to remember who we are. Life is very much a challenge, more so than we realize. It's a spiritual challenge, especially on this planet. In fact, many souls don't want to come here because of the preponderance of dark energy, which can manifest as evil."

Someone raised their hand in the audience, and I paused and pointed towards them.

"If life is divinely ordered and perfect, why does evil exist and flourish? This seems like a contradiction."

I nodded. "Let's see if I can clarify the apparent contradiction of evil and perfection. When you infringe upon another's will, you are breaking God's law. God doesn't care if you break God's law. There is no judgment. God simply reacts. God perceives a law is broken and, voila, evil breaks out.

"Notice that evil is live spelled backward. When we don't know how to live correctly, God reveals that we are living backward and manifests disharmony. Thus, instead of living in harmony, we experience disharmony. Evil is a play on words about the duality of this civilization. Live represents the word positive. Evil represents the word negative. Either is a choice that God allows, although negative choices create negative karma.

"Here's another minor point. When we are not behaving our best, we are infringing upon the will of others. This is where karma comes in. If we infringe on the will of others, God keeps score. This is done in the Akashic records, which I mentioned earlier. No one gets away with anything. Most lives are spent working off karma from past lives.

"This karma is not from God's judgment, but our own. We realize where we went awry and choose experiences to get us back on track.

"When we truly love God, we live accordingly. If we live correctly, we prevent karma from accumulating. Living correctly means loving and honoring others and ourselves – living by God's laws. We do this to make sure that we are growing. Eventually, we come to learn that the

Chapter Five - The Speech

first thing we must do is serve humanity. But remember, if someone else isn't serving humanity, it isn't for us to judge. We need to focus on our journey and to be an example.

"What does it mean to serve? That's for each of us to figure out. For me, it means following my heart and trying to accomplish my mission, which is figuring out why God put me on this planet. It also means helping others and living by example. I consider myself a soldier of God, but with no allegiance to any group except humanity. I only listen to my heart for orders, which is connected to God.

"Service is one of the highest forms of spirituality and implies spiritual awareness. If we are serving, it is likely that we are learning and growing. So, life isn't a party, and we aren't here to focus on having fun. We came to give ourselves to others. Yes, we can live with joy, realizing that we are an eternal soul. At the same time, life isn't meant to be easy. Life is about serving, learning, and growing.

"The people on this planet are now becoming aware of God on a mass scale. Thus, we should all be focusing on who we are. Not in a haphazard way, but in a serious manner. It's time to become aware of our divinity. Once we begin to have an awareness of who we are, we will stop forcing our will upon others. We will allow people to live their lives as they see fit.

"It may appear that many people will not change, but that simply isn't true. Once the majority of us become aware of who we are, we will release a love so powerful that others will change. It's inevitable. Others will change, and that will transform humanity. Once enough people become aware of their divinity, the world will become a better place.

"I have a feeling that the time is approaching when this will happen. I think that's why I'm here. Maybe I'm here to spur you on, to help you over that last hurdle. I hope so."

I paused for several seconds. "Are there any questions?"

A man rose from his seat. "Are you saying that all we have to do is be an example? We shouldn't try to instigate change?"

"No, I think you should instigate change. Tell the Chinese you are ready for a more harmonious society based on oneness and that repression is no longer acceptable. At first, they will ignore you, but keep it up." Many laughed. "Also, I think we can have as much of an impact by our beliefs as by our actions. Our example alone can have a major impact, as those who we come into contact with us are influenced by our beliefs."

He nodded and sat down.

"The mass consciousness of what we collectively believe determines society. If the majority exudes love, then we will be amazed at the amount of love that enters into everyone's life. Everyone is affected by those around them. If the majority of individuals radiate love, others cannot help but be influenced. We help love grow, not by seeking to change others, but by allowing others to be themselves. Radiate love. That's my advice. And tell the Chinese you want your freedom."

Several people laughed.

I smiled. "Thank you for coming. That's all for tonight." After a slight pause, everyone stood and applauded. I humbly nodded.

I walked off the platform and was met by a group of people. Many shook my hand and thanked me for coming. I smiled, and warmly accepted their appreciation. After a

Chapter Five - The Speech

few minutes, people began dispersing and walking up the aisles. Only a smattering of people remained.

Anderson introduced me to the short man from Denver. "Robinson is highly respected in the Underground. Many consider him to be the true leader."

"I don't," Robinson replied, as we shook hands. "I guess I'm in charge of the Colorado area, but nothing more. It's not something I sought; it just happened. People look to me to make decisions, and I've accepted that role."

Robinson intrigued me. He was incredibly calm. Nothing seemed to affect him. The only way I can describe him is that he was in love with everybody. He truly cared for those in his presence. Even after knowing him for a short time, I couldn't imagine him ever getting upset. His serenity was beyond anything I had ever experienced.

"Your speech was wonderful," he said. "I've been waiting a long time to hear it."

Here we go again, I thought. "The prophecy?"

"Actually, I saw you give it in a vision I had several years ago. Almost exactly as it occurred tonight, right here in this hall."

I smiled. "That's interesting. Have you had any other visions of the future?"

"Sure, I have them all the time. What you did tonight is only the beginning. Changes are starting to happen now. I could tell you what I expect to happen, but I prefer to keep my visions to myself. Sometimes they don't come to pass, and I don't want to lead people astray."

I nodded, accepting his explanation.

He looked into my eyes. "There are others who could have given your speech tonight, but it wouldn't have had the same effect. You've been prophesied for generations.

People have been waiting for you. Now events will lead to other events, and freedom will follow."

"Yes, that's the feeling I get. I'm here because it's time."

"Yes, it's time."

I nodded. "In my lifetime, I wanted to expose people to spiritual truth, but unless people were open to the message, it was a waste of effort. Most people weren't ready for the truth."

He nodded. "Yes, that's understandable. During your lifetime, there were people who were enlightened and tried to get the world to pay attention, but only a few listened."

"Do you remember any of their names?"

He shrugged his shoulders and made a face. "I can't remember, but that's where our spiritual philosophy came from. The New Agers of your generation."

He paused. "Oh yeah, Neale Walsch, he wrote the *Conversations With God* books, and Eckhart Tolle. Those two come to mind."

I smiled. "I read their books."

I looked around the theater. It was empty, except for Anderson, Henderson, Robinson, and myself. Anderson and Henderson had been silent as Robinson and I talked. I looked at Anderson and asked, "Do you know much about the originators of your spiritual philosophy?"

He looked at me with contemplation, then spoke. "Names aren't as important as the material. Robinson has shared his material with me, and I've read most of what he's read. The originators appear to be from your lifetime. People began to accept the concept of oneness in the late 20th century. It became widely known shortly thereafter."

"Amazing," I said. "I was alive when it started, and now it appears to be coming to fruition."

Chapter Five - The Speech

Anderson smiled. "The people were ready for your speech tonight. I don't know how to explain this, but they were waiting for it. Notice how everyone left? Why? Because they don't have any questions. All they needed from you was verification that you are authentic. Very few of them came here tonight to learn about spirituality. They came here to find out if the time has come."

"They got their answer," Robinson said.

We all smiled and walked to the exit.

Chapter Six

Colorado

The next day, Anderson, Robinson, and I flew to Denver. We were met at the airport by a government van. Robinson knew the Chinese driver who picked us up.

"Deng, are we going straight to Ouray?" Robinson asked the driver, as we drove out of the airport.

"Yes, sir. I have already loaded the van with the supplies you requested."

Robinson nodded, then looked at Anderson and me. "Ouray is where I live. It's located in a small canyon in the Rocky Mountains. It's safe, and you both can stay there as long as you want. It's the base camp for the Underground in this area. The people who live there are working to get our country back."

"How is it safe?" I asked. "The Chinese don't bother you?"

Robinson shook his head. "The earth changes devastated the western portion of the United States. The Chinese pretty much stay on the other side of the continental divide."

"So, Ouray is a kind of sanctuary?" I asked.

Robinson nodded. "You will love it."

I paused. There was silence as we drove toward the mountains.

"You said that you are working to get the country back. What exactly are you doing?" I asked.

"Well, as you know, we don't condone any form of violence. In fact, we inform the Chinese of people we know to be terrorists. Our goal is for the Chinese to acknowledge America as our own country and to give it back to us. We use subtle forms of persuasion, such as non-sanctioned – illegal – periodicals that inform Americans of our stance on issues. We persuade with ideas. For instance, we recommend not working for the Chinese and not cooperating. We try to make it as uncomfortable for the Chinese as possible."

Deng looked at me and smiled. "I love it when they whine," he said, in perfect English.

"Deng has been helping us for a couple of years," Robinson said. "He knows oppression is wrong and wants it to stop. It's only a matter of time before it's no longer a tenable course of action by the Chinese."

Through the windshield, we saw the Denver skyline and the Rocky Mountains in the background. There was very little traffic on the freeway, which was in surprisingly good shape.

"Is that all you do?" I asked Robinson. "Publish periodicals?"

"No," Robinson said. "Recently, we've started a program with highly evolved children. We have special children in Ouray who can leave their bodies and materialize in other locations."

"What?" I said, startled by the news.

Deng smiled a mischievous grin.

"Yeah, it's amazing," Robinson said. "We just started it, and I think you can help us. I can't wait for the children to meet you. You will inspire them."

Chapter Six - Colorado

"In what way?" I asked.

"What you said in your speech in Chicago is exactly what we are doing. We are asking the Chinese politely to leave. We are asking them to give us back our country so we can live in harmony. We are imploring them to do the right thing."

I nodded, thinking of the possibilities.

"Right now," Robinson continued, "the children aren't sure if it is morally the right thing to do. With their precociousness, they are very keen on human rights and fairness. Your presence will be interpreted as a sign that they should do this. The children are very loving and non-confrontational. They aren't sure we should be scaring the Chinese."

"Scaring them? How exactly is it being done?" I asked, intrigued.

"The children are materializing in the homes of the Chinese leaders and asking them politely to go home. We are telling them that their time here has come to a completion."

Anderson interjected. "With their superstitious nature, the Chinese just might leave."

"It sounds like guerrilla warfare without weapons.," I said, thinking out loud. "That might work."

"Yes, it might," Robinson said. "We're optimistic. The first few times we tried it, the Chinese were terrified. The children didn't know how to react and left without saying anything."

"How long have you been doing this?" I asked.

"About two months. We have four children who can do it, and more are learning. You both can help me run the operation. We need to plan carefully how to proceed. Currently, I'm targeting twelve Chinese officials in Omaha.

The children visit them on Saturday nights between two A.M. and three A.M. with a specific message."

"Wow," I said. "That's amazing. What's the message?"

"Currently, I'm having them say, '*You have to leave. It is time to give America back to its citizens.*' I've started with a short message. Soon, we'll change it to something more specific. At some point, we'll let them know that the Underground is behind this. I'd like you both involved, if possible. I'd like you both to remain in Ouray for a few months. It's your choice, but I could use your help."

I looked at Anderson.

Anderson looked at Robinson. "Let's meet the children and learn more about the program. Then we'll decide."

"Fair enough," Robinson said.

"I have an idea," I said. "After the Chinese begin complaining to Beijing, you can target officials there as well. Otherwise, China won't believe them or take it seriously. The decision to leave will not be made in this country."

Robinson nodded. "I like that. You are right. The final decision will be made in China."

"Have you thought about other demands?" I asked. "Right now, you're asking them to leave. Why not demand only part of the country? Try to negotiate with them. They understand the art of negotiating. We can give them everything east of the Kansas/Colorado border and keep the West. There isn't much western land since the earth shift. The Chinese might consider it a bargain, since they get legitimate ownership of the eastern portion of America. It would solve a lot of their political problems."

I waited for Robinson to respond.

Robinson contemplated. "We get West America, and we give them legitimate sovereignty of East America?

Chapter Six – Colorado

I hadn't thought of that. Can you imagine the euphoria if we can get them to agree? That would be an excellent first step. So what if we give them sovereignty? It's only a matter of time before all of humanity comes together in harmony. That could speed up the whole process. I like it."

"I agree," Anderson said. "Let's try it."

We arrived in Ouray eight hours later. We didn't see any Chinese soldiers in the mountains. The last hour was slow and bumpy, while we traversed a rutted dirt road to their location. It was located in a large canyon that was surrounded by steep mountains on three sides, like a diamond. It was a majestic location. As we drove into town, a park caught my attention. It was late afternoon, and children were playing. I was surprised by their vibrancy and happiness. There were families and several friendly dogs. Everyone was having a good time.

"People here appear happy," I said.

"Ouray is a special place," Robinson replied. "We have many evolved children here. Families with these special children travel here in secret from all over the country. It's the children who create the atmosphere. Wait until you meet them."

"How are these children different?" I asked.

"Their DNA is different from ours. Whereas we have two strands of DNA, they have multiple strands. Many of these children have special abilities. They are telepathic, telekinetic, clairvoyant, clairaudient, clairsentient, and often have other abilities, such as healing or higher intelligence. Their abilities don't tell the whole story, though. Most of them are old souls who are highly spiritually aware. Some remember their past lives, and all of them have a high ideal of humanity. Love is second nature to them. It's almost as if they only know how to love. Nothing else is important to them."

"How old are they?" I asked.

"The oldest one in Ouray is fourteen. These special children are becoming more common every year. We keep hearing about more of them who want to come here. Some of them are incredible healers. They can see auras and spot imbalances immediately. They can rebalance our energy and heal almost any ailment."

"Wow," I said. "And the children shall lead them...."

"What?" Anderson asked.

"It's a prophecy in the Bible," I said.

We parked on the main street. There weren't many vehicles, but the town was noticeably active. Almost every building had signs of life.

"How many people live here?" I asked.

"About five hundred," Robinson replied. "Everyone knows each other, and everyone works for the Underground."

We walked into a building and were quickly mobbed by those inside.

"They're here!" exclaimed the first person to see us.

Soon, everyone in the room surrounded us at the entrance. At least 20 people were waiting for us. They were excited to see us and met us with warm smiles. Robinson greeted friends and shook many hands. We made our way into the room and found a place to sit.

"Many of you may recognize Anderson's name." Robinson motioned toward Anderson, sitting next to him. "He's been instrumental in the Underground for over thirty years. Everyone, make sure he feels at home. He's lived in the prison in San Antonio for thirty years, and he could use some hospitality. This other gentleman," Robinson

Chapter Six - Colorado

motioned to me, "is from the past. This is John Randall. He was born in 1960, in California. He was cryogenically preserved in 1994 and recently revived by the Chinese. Unbeknownst to them, he will be our salvation."

Anderson smiled, and the others from Ouray also smiled. There was an outpouring of emotion directed at me.

Robinson looked at me. "Before I left, I told everyone why I was going to Chicago. I told everyone about you, and that I would try to bring you back. We're excited that you are with us, John. We want you to stay and make this your home. It's your choice, but I think this is probably the best place you could be. We're in the forefront. We make most of the decisions that are carried out by the Underground. This small community is the heart of the Underground."

Robinson paused, and the room was quiet. Everyone courteously listened to him. It was evident that he was in charge, and no one was going to interrupt him.

"You can have an impact here," Robinson said to me. "We know you're a writer, and we can see to it that you have a column published monthly. You can write from anywhere, but you'll be safer here. Also, I would like to put you in charge of the new program with the children. You have better ideas than I do, and your passion is strong. You're not afraid of the Chinese, and they will fear you. You're the right person for the job."

I didn't see any reason to leave Ouray. Where would I go? And I was very interested in the new program.

"I don't want to be in charge of the program," I answered. "I'd prefer that Anderson and I share that responsibility with you. I'd prefer a partnership."

I looked at Anderson, remembering what was said on the drive from Denver. "That is, if we like it here."

"A partnership would be perfect," Robinson said. "Stay a few weeks, and then decide if you want to stay on."

I looked at Anderson. He smiled and nodded.

"Okay," I said. "That's fine with us. Thank you. And thank you for treating Anderson and me like family. We're very grateful."

Robinson smiled. "The honor is ours. Thank you for staying with us."

"It's beautiful outside," I said. "Can we go back to that park? I'd love to walk on the grass, pet the dogs, and see the children."

"Sure," he said, getting up. "Let's go right now." He motioned to a friend of his. "Jimmy, can you bring some bottled water and sandwiches? We just made a long trip."

Jimmy nodded and hurried out the front door.

"Let's go," Robinson said to everyone in the room. "We can all walk."

Robinson led the way. We walked down Main Street in a large group, with everyone in the room joining us. The buildings that we passed were old but in good shape. They had been remodeled over the years. Most of the buildings were wood, with a coat of fresh paint. The people in Ouray obviously respected their community and took care of it. This also was evident by the lack of debris and trash. The streets and sidewalks were clean.

Once we arrived at the park, I felt rejuvenated. The sun was warm in a cloudless, bright blue sky. The grass that covered the park was emerald green, fragrant, and soft to the touch. I looked around, listened to the birds sing, and smiled. Normalcy had returned.

A little girl about seven years old with curly, long red hair ran up to me.

Chapter Six – Colorado

"Why are you smiling?" she asked.

"Because it's so beautiful here."

She laughed. "I know. Come meet my dog, Daisy."

I walked over with her to see her dog, a beautiful Golden Retriever. I got down on my knees and scratched Daisy's ears. "You sure have a nice dog. You are very lucky."

"I know. Are you staying with us? I haven't seen you before?"

"I'm visiting. What's your name?"

"Piper. What's yours?"

"John."

"You're here to help. My sister's been talking about you."

I smiled. "What has she been saying?"

"You're the man who wasn't born here. You're supposed to help us."

"Do you believe her?"

"Yeah, my sister's always right."

I looked into Piper's innocent blue eyes. "It was nice meeting you, Piper."

Piper and her dog walked back to her older sister.

I looked at Robinson. "I find it amazing that such a young girl would recognize me. Your community must be very close-knit."

He nodded. "Yeah, we get together quite often. Everyone knows each other. Tonight, many of us will get together for dinner. You'll see a lot of new faces."

* * * * *

An old food distribution center had been converted into the town meeting place. The tall ceiling made everything inside seem small. The rows and rows of tables and chairs in the cavernous building were too numerous to count. The building appeared to hold the entire town.

About a hundred people stood in line for the potluck. I was surprised by how much food they had. In addition to several cooks, people also came with food. Several tables held an assortment of choices. The food smelled delicious as the aroma circulated inside the building.

"Every Saturday night we have a potluck like this," Robinson said. "Everyone in town comes. It's a social gathering. We eat and talk. It usually starts at seven and ends around eleven."

"I notice that no one is smoking or drinking alcohol. Is that a rule?" I asked.

Robinson nodded. "We allow people to do as they wish in private, but in public, we have decided to ban drugs. We don't even serve caffeine. We want to set an example for the children."

"As our society has become more spiritual," Anderson added, "people have become more concerned with their health. What they do here in Ouray is common throughout the country. There are many vegetarians here, and meat consumption is very low."

We got in line, along with several of Robinson's friends. I loaded my plate with vegetables, rice, and bread. It looked incredibly good. Then, the group of us found a table and relaxed.

Robinson sat down across from me, savored a few bites, and then spoke thoughtfully. "Tomorrow would be a good day for you and Anderson to meet the children. They are coming over to my house in the morning. We can discuss your ideas with them."

Chapter Six – Colorado

He said 'we,' but I got the impression that he wanted me to talk to the children.

"I would like that very much," I said.

Many people came by our table to introduce themselves and say hello to Anderson and me. Some of them sat down at our table and talked. They asked Anderson about San Antonio, and me about America, long ago. We answered all of their questions and enjoyed the evening.

Robinson was right – we did meet many new people. The community was well-educated and well-informed. We didn't really talk about spiritual matters, although I could tell that they were already spiritually aware by their extraordinary calmness and gentle demeanor.

* * * * *

We stayed with Robinson. He lived alone in a three-bedroom house. If we decided to stay long-term, there were other houses like his available, which had been empty for years. We could remodel a house and stay there permanently.

In the morning, the children began arriving. They knocked politely on Robinson's front door, and I let them in. I introduced myself and asked them their names and ages. They answered my questions, then headed to the back, where Robinson had built a large room for meetings and for hosting friends.

The back room was cozy. It was clean and well-vacuumed, with wall-to-wall carpeting. The children enjoyed sitting on it. There were several sofas and chairs to sit on as well. Wood paneling covered the walls. Two skylights were in the roof, with windows on three walls, provided plenty of light.

As usual, Robinson was in charge, and everyone deferred to him. "Kids, these are my friends, John and Andy. They're here to help us. They're going to stay with me and attend our meetings. Hopefully, they'll choose to stay and live with us in Ouray. I want each of you to introduce yourselves and describe your abilities. Tell them what you can do … anything you want to talk about. If you have any questions for them, they'll be happy to answer."

An attractive woman walked into the room, carrying a plate of freshly baked chocolate chip cookies that smelled delicious. The children were excited to see her. She was in her late 20s, with short blonde hair and a clear complexion. I knew immediately that I wanted to meet her.

She said hello to the children first, then to everyone else, as she walked to a table and set down the plate.

"Hello, Julie," Robinson said. "How are you?"

"I'm fine. Sorry I'm late."

She found a seat across the room from us.

"This is John and Andy. They're going to be working with us."

"Nice to meet you," she said.

I smiled. "Hi."

Robinson said to Anderson and me, "Julie helps train the children with their gifts. She's an excellent teacher and highly instrumental to our goals."

He said to Julie, "The children were just starting to introduce themselves to John and Andy."

Then he turned to the four children. "Let's start with this side of the room. Josh, you go first."

The children were between nine and 14. The youngest age allowed in the project was nine, which seemed young for what they were being asked to do. However, these were evolved children who showed enormous maturity.

Chapter Six – Colorado

Josh was 12 years old but talked like an adult. He was sure of himself and did not like to be treated as a child.

Josh began. "I started remembering my past life when I was three. I was on a planet called Aza, in the Pleiades constellation. Aza orbited two suns and had three moons. I remember Aza very well. I was an architect who built homes designed for several families to live together. The homes were more like small, enclosed communities. We used clear plastic domes to protect us from the ultraviolet sunlight. We wore protective clothing and eye shields when we went outside. Everyone was nice to each other. There was no violence or hatred, and everyone got along well. I had a family and two children. I could talk about this for a long time, but it's time for someone else."

From my place on a sofa, I said, "Wait, I have a few questions. Do you feel like you brought your beliefs about God with you from your past life? And can you share some of those beliefs?"

He nodded. "Of course. I remember that I am one with God, that we are all *one consciousness*. My mission in this life is to be a conscious instrument of the divine presence and to spread the light. And to always remember that unity begins with self-love and gratitude is the only path to love."

"Thank you," I said, then asked the other children, "Do all of you agree with Josh? Do you all feel like you are one with God?"

They all smiled and nodded. It was a beautiful moment. In this room, filled with enlightened children, I suddenly knew that the world *would* transform. I also sensed that the level of awareness in this room existed elsewhere on the planet. There were other children like these, and their voices would also be heard.

I asked Josh another question. "I know that you can leave your body and materialize at any location on the planet. What other abilities do you have?"

"Same as the others," he replied matter-of-factly. There was no tone of ego, or implication that he felt special or unusual. To these children, their gifts were natural. "I'm telepathic, telekinetic, clairvoyant, and lots of other things. I'm good at healing. I healed my brother's twisted ankle last week. I can hear other people's thoughts. Stuff like that."

"Thank you," I said. I scanned the children, looking into their eyes. The level of intelligence that I perceived was stunning. "Do any of you feel uncomfortable visiting the Chinese in your ethereal bodies?"

After a pause, Sarah, a sweet 13-year-old with long, black, straight hair, spoke. "We want to help. We understand how important it is to get our country back so that we can create peace on Earth."

I nodded. "Do you think what we are trying to do is morally correct? Do you think it's the right thing to do?"

She nodded. "We're trying to show them that God wants us to live in freedom. I don't like it when we scare them, but we can't help that."

Elizabeth, sitting next to Sarah, asked, "How can it be wrong to use God's gifts? If they were treating us fairly, we wouldn't have to scare them." She was the oldest at 14 and the leader of the children. In many ways, she saw herself as the protector of the other children on the team.

I nodded. "Very well said, and I agree completely. Do all of you agree with Sarah and Elizabeth?"

They all nodded.

I smiled. "Good, me, too. I have some ideas. We're going to try to free Colorado. How does that sound?"

Chapter Six - Colorado

They all smiled and clapped. They were a confident bunch.

"Is it true that you weren't born here?" Elizabeth asked.

All of the children stared at me, waiting for the answer.

I nodded, and the children became excited. Their eyes and expressions implied that they wanted me to tell them more.

"I was born west of here, in a state called California, long before it fell into the ocean and became a series of tiny islands."

"When?" asked Sam, an inquisitive nine-year-old, wearing thick glasses, and looking nerdy.

"1960."

"Wow. How old are you?" he asked.

I smiled at his excitement. "I'm thirty-four, but I feel different since I woke up a few weeks ago. I feel younger now."

"How did you wake up?" Sarah asked. "Were you asleep?"

"No, cryogenically suspended."

"What is that?" she asked.

"It's when a doctor freezes your body and stores you safely in a special location. I wouldn't recommend it, though. You never know what year you'll wake up."

The kids laughed.

"How did you get in prison with Anderson?" Josh asked.

"I think the universe put me there so I could meet all of you, and we could help the planet."

There was a short silence, as the children stared at me.

Sarah said, "You talk like we do."

I smiled. "Yeah, we have a lot in common. For instance, we all know that we have an eternal soul and that this planet is not our true home. We know that gratitude is false unless it leads to virtue. We know that the more we love ourselves, the more it will be reflected back. We know that the higher we align with our higher self, the more we shine our light to the world."

They nodded.

I let them continue with their introductions, and each child introduced him or herself. They were mature and eager to carry out the program that Robinson and Julie had begun.

After the introductions, Robinson stood. "John and Andy are going to help Julie and I with your program. I'm excited they are here to help us. It was John's idea to ask the Chinese to leave Colorado and give them the eastern portion of the United States. John and Andy have come up with a plan to accomplish this. I'll let John explain it."

Robinson sat. I stood and walked over to a whiteboard on one of the walls. I picked up a blue pen on the tray under the board and wrote:

> I have three things to say:
>
> 1. We want our freedom back.
>
> 2. We will leave you alone, if you leave us alone.
>
> 3. Are you willing to negotiate?

I turned and faced the children. "This is going to be your new message. Each of you memorize it and practice

Chapter Six - Colorado

saying it to each other. You will give your new message next Saturday night beginning at two A.M. We will continue each week until we get an answer of yes or no."

The children looked at me inquisitively and enthusiastically. They precociously understood the importance of what they were trying to do. I was surprised by their commitment.

I continued. "We have selected the twelve highest Chinese officials in Omaha. Each of you will be assigned three officials. We want you to become friends with your officials. Be nice to them. Treat them as if they were your little brother or sister. Be gentle and loving."

"How do we do that?" Sarah asked.

"Right now, when you appear to the Chinese officials, they don't understand who you are. It's like with a newborn child. The child isn't sure of their mother but learns over time. With a baby, we are very gentle and loving, waiting for them to grow. We have to do the same with the Chinese officials. We don't want them to be afraid. We want them to listen and to trust us."

The children nodded.

"Over time, the Chinese officials will come to know you and not be afraid. If you can become a friend, it will help us to form a dialogue with them. That is our goal. We want to sit down with them and negotiate an agreement to split the country in two. We could ask them to leave the entire country, but why be greedy and get nothing? If we give them legitimate sovereignty over more than half the country, I think they will agree to give us the rest."

"Oh, boy, this is good," Josh blurted out, unable to control his enthusiasm.

The kids laughed, and we adults smiled.

I continued. "After a few weeks, we expect that the Chinese leaders in China will be watching you deliver your messages through cameras. Hopefully, they will want to negotiate. Once they understand we have this kind of power, they should want to talk."

"Why?" Elizabeth asked. "Why will they want to talk?"

"Because of fear, but also because of pragmatism," I said. "We are offering to leave them alone and give them the eastern portion of this country. We are also offering them an end to the resistance, and an end to the Underground movement. But, more importantly, we are offering them legitimacy. For the first time since they took control of America by force, we are offering them legal ownership."

"Wow," Josh said. "We're making history."

I smiled. "Yes, I think we are."

The children all smiled.

"Hopefully, we'll negotiate with the Chinese to leave the western portion of the United States and never come back. Everything west of the Colorado/Kansas border will be West America. That's the goal. It will be our new country. We will be free."

The children all clapped their hands and laughed.

"How long will it take?" Elizabeth asked.

"I expect it to take a while, perhaps a month or two."

They were silent.

Elizabeth asked, "If they agree to let us have West America, are we going to let them keep East America?"

"Yes, that's the plan. We'll give them East America, in exchange for West America."

"Do you think it will work?" Sarah asked.

Chapter Six - Colorado

"Yes, I do. I think they'll do it if they trust us to leave them alone."

"Why should we give them half of our country?" Elizabeth asked.

I smiled. "It's only short-term. They don't realize that the world is changing spiritually at an incredible rate. As each day passes, more and more highly evolved children are being born. This raises the vibration of the planet, and will cause the Chinese to lose their power. If the Chinese give us the West, it's only a matter of time before East and West unite in peace. In a sense, we're not really letting them keep East America. It just appears that way in the short-term."

Josh's eyes lit up. "Yes, that's what's going to happen! If we are living in peace in the West, they won't be able to ignore our love and harmony. They'll want it, too. We'll be an example they can't deny. Eventually, they'll come to emulate us, then join us as one!"

The children all nodded.

"We get to free the world," Elizabeth said, in an awed tone.

"You get to help," I said. "What you are doing is possible because of all who have come before you. The process of spiritual enlightenment on this planet has been a slow process over generations. You are a privileged bunch. You get to do the final act."

"That's what Elizabeth meant," Sarah said.

"I know. I think all of you know you are part of a team – God's team."

"That's what I meant," Elizabeth said.

"Indeed, sweet," I said. "I think all of you understand your responsibility. You have to work hard and be smart. This is a serious undertaking."

"We know how important it is," Josh said.

I paused. "I want to tell all of you something about yourselves that you may not already know. Being able to materialize your body elsewhere means that you are highly evolved. Leaving the body is common, but materializing it elsewhere is rare and not easily achieved. It means that you have lived many past lives and have developed a high spiritual awareness. With this awareness comes a responsibility.

"You are here on this planet, at this time, because you can have a positive impact. You have a spiritual awareness that can help this planet. How you use your awareness is up to you, but I hope you will attempt to uplift humanity. The ultimate lifestyle is to live your lives knowing that you are helping humanity. Each of you has the ability to do that."

"How do we do that?" Sam asked.

"Study spirituality and metaphysics until you find your life path – the reason why you are here. After that, it's just a matter of following your heart and letting your life unfold.

"The one thing you want to guard against is your ego controlling you. The ego exists in your head when you think about the past or the future. The ego does not exist in the present moment. So, to marginalize the ego, you want to stay in the present moment. The present moment is the gateway to your higher self and your intuition. You want to open that channel and keep it open. By staying in the present moment, magical things can happen since you are in alignment with your higher self.

"Let me give you an example. Neil Young, a musician during my lifetime, was considered a musical genius. But he was also considered eccentric for his behavior and

Chapter Six - Colorado

decisions. Later in life, he said that the reason he made his decisions was that he was following his muse. He said he honored his intuition, no matter what the consequences.

"He was prone to making snap decisions that others questioned. For instance, one time he tried to make a movie for an entire year, even though he didn't know what he was doing. Other times, he would quit bands or quit tours unexpectedly. Once, he made a record that nobody wanted to hear and was sued by his record company. This was his typical behavior, and he never questioned his decisions. He said that, if an idea came to him, and it was still there the next day, he acted on it.

"Neil was his own man, and he made his own decisions. He followed his inspiration, instead of letting others or society dictate his decisions. His example is a great lesson of how we need to be true to our feelings and intuition. He showed us how guiding ourselves is the best way to live our lives. By following his muse, he became one of the greatest rock musicians of all time and, more importantly, very satisfied with his life."

"Did he have long hair?" Sarah asked.

I smiled. "Most of his life, he did. Why?"

"My brother said the rock stars all had long hair."

I smiled. "Okay, get out of here. Go have some fun."

The kids jumped to their feet and headed through the door, picking up cookies on their way out.

Julie walked over and stood near Robinson, Anderson, and me. "John, that was great. The children really like you."

As she spoke, I could feel my attraction to her.

She continued. "These kids are very smart and exceptionally mature. I have conversations with them like they're adults. They're usually bored with adults because they're so smart, but you had their attention."

"Thank you," I said. "I noticed when you walked in that you have a strong relationship with the children. They were excited to see you."

"They're my students ... and my friends," she said nonchalantly. "I get along well with them."

Robinson said, "The kids love her. Julie is their mentor."

I looked at her with respect and admiration. "I understand you've been teaching them to project their bodies."

"I teach them many things. You can come to our classes if you want."

"I'd like that," I said, trying to contain my excitement.

"Can I come, too?" Anderson asked.

"Of course," she said.

Julie sat down on the sofa next to Robinson. "I have a question, John. When you told the kids, you are one with God, what did you mean?"

"You know the answer."

"Yes, but I want to know what it means to you."

I smiled. "We're all fragments of a whole, which is God. We are individual souls, yet we exist as a collective. If we make a decision, it affects the entire collective. All individual beings in the entire collective are actually one. We are all interconnected. The connecting link is the consciousness of God. Whereas we think we have an individual consciousness, in fact, we all share the same consciousness."

I paused. "Is that enough?"

She laughed. "No. I want the long answer."

Chapter Six - Colorado

I smiled. "Okay. This shared consciousness is why compassion and loving kindness is the most powerful thought we can have. Compassion and loving kindness allow us to be our true self. It allows us to recognize our connection to others ..."

"The collective," she interrupted.

"Exactly. To create harmony, we need to base our lives on the fact that we are all one. Otherwise, we would live with the false belief of separation, and that causes disharmony and trauma ..."

"Conversely," she interrupted, "if we are aware of the collective, we can have harmony. Being responsible for myself, I'm being responsible for all. By honoring you, I'm honoring all, of which I am a part."

"Very good," I said, somewhat surprised by Julie's spiritual awareness. "To honor is also to do no harm. The Essenes, who taught Jesus, called this being harmless, which was one of the highest values they held. Conversely, if I harm you, I also harm myself. Moreover, if I harm myself, I harm the collective, which harms everyone."

She smiled mischievously. "If everything is a collective, then how can we exist as individuals? How can we be real if we're part of a collective?"

"It doesn't matter if we have a personal identity and exist as individuals. What matters is that we are one with God. Our true identity is that of God. We are the whole."

"I am that I am?" she asked.

"Exactly."

"We surrender to the whole at the expense of our individuality," Julie said.

"Yes. That's what enlightenment is all about. It's not really surrendering. Instead, it is an awareness that the whole is more real than the individual. This is why Josh said his mission in this life is to be a conscious instrument of the divine presence. Does that make sense?"

She nodded. "Yes, I'm just testing you, John. Keep going, I'm enjoying this."

I had a feeling that she already knew everything I was explaining. However, my attraction to her evaporated any frustration I felt at explaining something she already knew. If she wanted me to prove that I was her equal, that was fine with me.

"We have to become aware that individuality is an illusion. The whole is the reality. In fact, the only blasphemy is the denial of the divine. Individual will, which comes from the ego, is what keeps us from enlightenment. We think we want to be individuals, but that isn't what we really want. Our ultimate goal is enlightenment, and individuality keeps us from attaining it."

Julie smiled. "If enlightenment is our goal, then what is the meaning of life?"

"To experience. To be. To remember who we are. To become spiritually aware. Any of these. When we remember we are the whole, individualism becomes an illusion. Thus, our goal and the meaning of life are essentially the same thing. You could say enlightenment is the meaning of life."

"Or spiritual awareness," she added.

"Yes. Spiritual growth is the reason we incarnate over and over. Until we become spiritually aware, we aren't satisfied. This drives us to become more aware. Everyone is searching for more awareness … even if they don't do it consciously."

"Everyone is learning about their true selves," she said.

Chapter Six - Colorado

"Yes. On a subconscious level, everyone wants enlightenment. The lack of enlightenment isn't satisfying. It creates frustration and leads us to seek satisfaction through the ego."

"We seek happiness through the ego until it is no longer satisfying?" she asked.

"Yes. We know there is joy in our soul, and we try to achieve it through individuation. We make choices to find joy. We get married, raise a family, succeed in business, and have hobbies. Where does it lead? To fulfillment? To enlightenment?"

"No," she said.

"That's right. Something is still missing, and that something is spiritual enlightenment. Satisfaction comes only through the awareness of our divine nature. Without that, we're frustrated."

Julie looked at me seriously. "That sounds good, but can anyone become enlightened by hearing these words? Isn't it difficult to become enlightened? Aren't frustration and the lack of satisfaction a part of life?"

I nodded. "Generally, yes. This is why we don't have to become enlightened in this lifetime. That's what reincarnation is for. All we have to do in this life is *be*. Be ourselves and live our lives. If that leads to enlightenment, great. If it doesn't, then that's okay, too. But, when this life is over, we'll plan the next one with the explicit intent of steadily reaching the goal of enlightenment. That's the ultimate destination."

"You're intense, John. I thought Robinson was intense."

Robinson and Anderson laughed.

I liked her and wanted to say something that would make her like me. "I'm not always serious. I have a playful side, too. My moon is in Sagittarius." I smiled.

"I think that means he likes you," Anderson said to Julie.

She smiled brightly.

*****

Word spread quickly about the children materializing to the Chinese officials in their ethereal light bodies. The haunting of the Chinese leadership was the talk of the country.

Word also spread about my prior speech in Chicago, and that I was working with the children and the Underground. A video file of my Chicago speech was distributed around the country. Thousands saw it. The Chinese found out about it and offered a large reward for my whereabouts.

We were making progress. And more and more people were talking about freedom. The new tone in the air had been missing for centuries.

The program had now been in place for one month. So far, the Chinese officials had not talked to the children during their materialized visits. The Chinese were listening to our messages, but they were not responding. They were hoping we would go away.

We decided to change our tactics to get a response. We released information in our Underground periodical, stating that the children would not stop until we negotiated a peace treaty to split the country in two. There would be a new free America in the west and the Chinese could have the east.

Chapter Six - Colorado

The tactic worked. Two weeks later, when Sarah made a visit, the frightened Chinese official told her they were ready to negotiate. As an act of faith, they would immediately withdraw from the northwestern states: Oregon, Washington, and Idaho.

They requested to negotiate with us in person. Anderson and Robinson didn't like the idea of us meeting them in person. However, Josh knew that it would be okay, and that the Chinese had already decided to accept our demand to give us everything west of the Colorado/Kansas border. They were afraid that we would spread our "visits" to China. They were ready to finalize the agreement.

In fact, Josh had remotely watched the Chinese discussing the matter in Beijing. Using remote viewing, he had watched and listened to their deliberations, and we knew exactly what the Chinese leaders were thinking.

We demanded that the Chinese government announce to the world that negotiations with the Underground were planned. And that the negotiations would focus on splitting the country in half. Once this was announced, we would meet with them.

Everyone in Ouray was ecstatic. We were finally on the verge of achieving our freedom. The children did one last visitation to tell Chinese leaders this would be the last visit. During the visit, many of the Chinese officials told the children that they would now be our friends. We would work together, East and West.

A week later, Robinson, Anderson, and I met with the Chinese leaders in a televised meeting in Denver. For this most auspicious event in centuries, we appeared in public, in front of cameras. We smiled while the Chinese leaders looked dour. It was our moment in history.

The actual negotiations took place behind closed doors. There were three days of painstaking discussions. The document was over 500 pages long and many of the details had to be discussed. The Chinese pretended not to speak English and used interpreters. We could not tell what they were discussing in Mandarin, and it was difficult to know if everything was proceeding in a positive manner. The Chinese meticulously went over the rules of their sovereignty of East America. They wanted our assurances that we clearly understood what was being signed and agreed to in the accord.

And then it was done. The Chinese upheld their end of the agreement and vacated all of the lands west of the Colorado/Kansas border.

After the water inundation in the 21st century, that didn't leave much. California, Nevada, Arizona, and Utah were mostly gone, leaving only Washington, Oregon, Idaho, Montana, Wyoming, Colorado and New Mexico. However, what was left was more than enough for a new beginning.

The Chinese began a widespread relocation program to transfer all Americans, including those in prison, to the Western states. People traveled by plane, bus, or smaller vehicles to regain their freedom.

West America had officially gained her independence, and a joyful, national celebration took place.

The East-West American Accord marked an incredible stepping stone towards the goal of world peace and establishing a new world civilization. But more importantly, for the first time in history, a major war had been fought without firing a single shot.

*****

Chapter Six - Colorado

After a short period of time, West America began to embrace the spirituality of oneness. Soon after, the love and peace that reigned in West America was emulated throughout the world. The spiritual awareness of the planet rose to a level where everyone was honored and respected as the literal embodiment of God. No longer were people forced to survive through competition. Now everyone was given the opportunity to do as they chose. Free choice and free will were the new foundational building blocks of humanity. And God's law of not forcing your will upon another became the new normal. The ultimate goal of creating a civilization based on love was achieved. And those souls who were around to experience this reality were incredibly grateful to all of those who came before them – us!

* * * * *

We were at the park having a picnic with all of the evolved children, celebrating our successful liberation of West America. Everyone from the team was there, sitting at picnic tables and eyeing the delicious food. At one table, Josh and Sam sat across from Sarah and Elizabeth. They were smiling, enjoying the beautiful weather. At another nearby table, Anderson, Robinson, Julie, and I sat.

I was across from Julie, and we continued to look at each other.

"Okay, John, who did the seating arrangement?" Julie asked.

I looked at Anderson and Robinson. "I didn't do it."

Anderson and Robinson laughed.

"Julie, stop playing hard to get and go out with him," Robinson said.

"He has to ask me first."

We all smiled.

Piper walked up with a rose and handed it to me. "Try this." She smiled and laughed.

www.ingramcontent.com/pod-product-compliance
Lightning Source LLC
Chambersburg PA
CBHW071928290426
44110CB00013B/1518